The Priory of Sion

Hoax,

Conspiracy,

or Secret Society?

Conrad Bauer

Copyrights

All rights reserved. © Conrad Bauer and Maplewood Publishing No part of this publication or the information in it may be quoted from or reproduced in any form by means such as printing, scanning, photocopying, or otherwise without prior written permission of the copyright holder.

Disclaimer and Terms of Use

Effort has been made to ensure that the information in this book is accurate and complete. However, the author and the publisher do not warrant the accuracy of the information, text, and graphics contained within the book due to the rapidly changing nature of science, research, known and unknown facts, and internet. The author and the publisher do not hold any responsibility for errors, omissions, or contrary interpretation of the subject matter herein. This book is presented solely for motivational and informational purposes only. The publisher and author of this book does not control or direct users' actions and are not responsible for the information or content shared, harm and/or action of the book readers. The presentation of the information is without contract or any type of guarantee assurance. This book is not meant to be used, nor should it be used, to diagnose or treat any medical condition. For diagnosis or treatment of any medical problem, consult your own physician. The publisher and author are not responsible for any specific health or allergy needs that may require medical supervision and are not liable for any damages or negative consequences from any treatment, action, application or preparation, to any person reading or following the information in this book. References, if any, are provided for informational purposes only and do not constitute endorsement of any websites or other sources. Readers should be aware that the websites listed in this book, if any, may change.

ISBN: 978-1535419666

Printed in the United States

Contents

Introduction 1
Hidden Evidence 3
The Secrets of The Holy Blood and the Holy Grail 23
The Royal Bloodline 35
A Growing Revolt 45
The Truth 51
The Victims of the Priory 59
The Fallout 71
    Mary Magdalen 72
    The Grand Masters 79
    The Da Vinci Code 85
Conclusion 89
Further Reading 93
About the Author 95
    More Books from Conrad Bauer 97

Introduction

Hoax, conspiracy, or secret society? That is the range of responses you might hear when raising the idea of the Priory of Sion. Ostensibly a clandestine order designed to disguise the truth about the children of Jesus Christ, the group have been labeled as either an elaborate concoction, or the most powerful secret society in the world. Are they real? What are they hiding? Where did they come from? What impact can they have on the world around us? These are the questions this book will hope to answer.

At the heart of the story of the Priory of Sion is the somewhat heretical notion that Jesus Christ — the supposed son of God — fathered children. Not only that, but that his bloodline survives to this day. If true, the idea has a huge impact on the very existence of Christianity, the world's most popular religion. If the Priory — as is believed — are guarding the truth about such a matter, they then potentially control some of the most powerful information in the world. Think of it like an ideological atomic bomb, ticking away and ready to explode through the consciousness of the world.

Not only that, but the men allegedly chosen to guard these secrets rank as some of the greatest thinkers in human history. Isaac Newton, Nicholas Flamel, and Leonardo da Vinci have all been implicated in the order, though their involvement is debated. In fact, the entire existence of the order has been argued. Some suggest that, rather than a secret society, the Priory is in fact an elaborate hoax.

Others claim that these accusations are merely an attempt to disguise the truth. But what do we know for certain? Who exactly are the Priory of Sion?

Hidden Evidence

One of the most important parts of this story is a battle. On one side is an American, pressed into defending himself. On the other side, three Englishmen stand convinced that they have been robbed and their ideas made to seem ridiculous. It is as though their honor has been sullied. They demand satisfaction. Each side is spending hundreds of thousands of dollars to face off against the other and it will not be settled until one side emerges victorious. But rather than some medieval fist fight or Victorian duel, this is a very recent battle. Though the history of the Priory of Sion is said to stretch back for thousands of years, this fight was fought after the turn of the second millennium. The venue is the Royal Courts of Justice in a part of London known as the Strand. The date is 2006.

This is where we will start. These days, it is impossible to discuss the Priory of Sion without mentioning a number of books. These books vary in popularity, from an international bestseller which made its author millions, through to a supposedly academic work which defied expectations and left a print on the world, and finally, an obscure French text, one which many people have credited with starting this entire affair. Appropriately enough for a story that may or may not be true, the publishing of books is inextricably linked to the Priory in every single respect. As we shall see, the writing, the reading, and the impact of these texts is essential to the story.

Of these books, two were written by the men who stood opposed to one another in the Strand. On one side was Dan Brown, writer of *The Da Vinci Code*, and the man often credited with turning the Priory of Sion into a global concern. Condemned by the Church, ridiculed by critics, his work has nevertheless proved to be a success beyond any comprehension. For the university professor, it has become a rich industry. As someone who teaches other to write, there are few people in the world better placed to tell others how to make money from a story. But how that story came to be is the entire predicament of the court case.

On the other side of the courtroom stand two men and their team of lawyers. Richard Leigh, hailing from New Jersey, and Michael Baigent, hailing from New Zealand. They glower at Dan Brown (who, strangely enough, hails from New Hampshire) from the other side of Court 61. Dan Brown is the defendant and the other two men have accused him of plagiarism. Brown, they say, not only stole their ideas, but presented them to the world in a way which discredited the work they had done. Baigent and Leigh are better known to the world as the authors of *The Holy Blood and the Holy Grail*. As well as being one of the most popular pieces of writing ever created on the subject of the Holy Grail, their book brings the idea of the Priory of Sion to an English-speaking audience. As we will discover soon, their work was wildly successful and few writers have come as close to delivering as ground-breaking, as controversial, and as profitable a take on religion in the last three centuries.

And so both sides of the courtroom are inhabited by writers. On this day, a verdict is to be reached which will lend credence to (or demolish the credibility of) an idea which is said to date back almost 2,000 years. At the heart of the matter, with the judge set to rule, is the purported existence of the Priory of Sion. Through the works of both sides of the argument, the Priory's name has reached more ears than anyone ever thought possible. While Brown has managed to dominate the bestseller charts in the world of fiction, Baigent and Leigh (as well as a third author who is not present, but who will be touched upon soon) created massive waves in the world of non-fiction. Between them, they have dominated both sides of the bestseller charts.

That is one of the key underlying aspects of the case and, by extension, the existence of the Priory of Sion itself. There is a huge amount of money to be made in publishing these ideas. Whether that is because they are dangerous, because they are revelatory, or because they are entertaining, is never really made clear. But, simply because the case ever came to court, there is money to be made through publishing works on the Priory of Sion. And, with court cases such as these, there is also a huge amount of money to be lost.

So what exactly were the duo of Baigent and Leigh claiming in Courtroom 61? Their case was not as simple as run-of-the-mill plagiarism. Typically, in plagiarism cases, the prosecution must prove that the defendant took their idea and made a profit on it, without attributing credit or sharing in the revenue. This has been done countless times in the past and, in the world of publishing (and the media at large) it is not uncommon. But this particular case was slightly different.

Specifically, Baigent and Leigh claimed that Brown — in *The Da Vinci Code* — made use of a plot that was "directly plagiarized" from their own book, *The Holy Blood and the Holy Grail*. Stealing this idea, they said, allowed Brown to make a huge amount of money from the ideas of the original authors. At the time of the court case, it was estimated that Brown's writing had made him in excess of $45 million. Besides the book, there was the multi-million dollar film franchise starring Tom Hanks. *The Da Vinci Code* had achieved huge success, ranking perhaps alongside Harry Potter alone in terms of post-millennial publishing successes. This success, the prosecution alleged, was built on top of ideas that were borrowed wholesale from *The Holy Blood and the Holy Grail*.

That is not to say that *The Holy Blood and the Holy Grail* had not been successful in its own right. Far from it. Indeed, after being published in the 1980s, the book caused a huge stir. But it was considered (by both its authors and its readership) as a work of non-fiction. Walk into any bookshop in a quest for the book and it would be found in the non-fiction section. Indeed, rather than the new age or the spirituality section, *The Holy Blood and the Holy Grail* was nestled amid other, weightier works under the banner of history. This was the realm in which the book dominated. Most non-fiction books do not sell in huge numbers, but this one was different. Perhaps because it managed to transition from the speculative theology that most people dismiss, into the realms of accepted historicism, it had become immensely popular.

And herein lay the rub. For the authors of *The Holy Blood and the Holy Grail*, the very existence of *The Da Vinci Code* undermined their own work. Not only were ideas borrowed from the historical text, but they were presented in a fictional world, and this brought them into question. Convinced as they were that the Priory of Sion was a real, functioning body, the way in which Dan Brown had taken and presented his ideas undid all of the work they had achieved to that point. Their future successes (and the successes of the sequels to *The Holy Blood and the Holy Grail*) were damaged by the existence of *The Da Vinci Code*. This was why they were suing.

To that point, it almost seemed as though money was far from the issue. Baigent, Leigh, and Henry Lincoln (the third writer) had already become wealthy men. Their years of research into what had eventually become *The Holy Blood and the Holy Grail* had turned them from struggling writers into authorities on the Holy Grail and, in particular, the Priory of Sion. Michael Baigent was even quoted at the time as having said, "Whether our hypothesis is right or wrong is irrelevant." The lawsuit was not an attempted to earn punitive damages, but to protect their ideas, to protect their integrity, and to protect the idea of the Priory of Sion. As Baigent stated, the authors felt as though they had "no choice."

Baigent and Leigh resented "being lumped in" with the work of fiction known as *The Da Vinci Code*. As they constantly insisted in the press, it seemed more and more as though this was indeed a high-minded quest to protect their intellectual property in the face of an overwhelming behemoth of the fictional world. It was almost as though these men were the protectors of the integrity of the Priory of Sion, holding out against the bastardized version that had been presented to the world by the callous Dan Brown. As anyone in the publishing world will tell you, a non-fiction bestseller (such as *The Holy Blood and the Holy Grail*) might net plaudits and respect, but a fiction bestseller (such as *The Da Vinci Code*) will always net you the profits. So while Baigent and Leigh were keen to protect their integrity and that of their work, Dan Brown and his publishers were very keen to keep their money-making avenues open. And so there the men found themselves, facing off against one another in a London courtroom.

Key to Baigent's argument (and that of his legal team) was the idea of "historical implication." *The Holy Blood and the Holy Grail*, the authors argued, was an authoritative historical text. It was one that they had spent years researching and putting together. *The Da Vinci Code*, if read by millions, damaged the implied historical accuracy of the non-fiction work. It was not quite plagiarism, but it was the argument that Baigent repeated time and time again in the press.

But the idea seemed to fly in the face of common sense. Surely, if a reader sat down with either book, they would naturally know that one was a work of fiction and the other was a work of non-fiction? The tone, presentation, style, and even the cover of the book would tell them as much. As long as *The Da Vinci Code* veered away from quoting verbatim tracts of the other text without crediting it, how could this "historical implication" affect *The Holy Blood and the Holy Grail*?

Furthermore, if the alleged history told by the authors of *The Holy Blood and the Holy Grail* was indeed held to be true, the facts should have been available to a fiction writer regardless of whether they appeared in a particular book or not. When writing about the past, school textbook writers rarely take authors to court over the mention of the Battle of Hastings or the Spanish Inquisition. If the book written by Baigent and his co-writers was based purely on fact (as is the premise in non-fiction) then there seemed little wrong with Dan Brown making use of an idea such as the Priory of Sion, and the secrets they guarded.

It took three weeks to reach a verdict. The judge assigned to the case, Peter Smith, seemed to be enjoying his moment in the limelight. Rarely in the British legal system, it seemed, was he allowed to partake in such a sensational but also so clear cut a case. It was no surprise when Judge Smith ruled in the favor of the defendant, Dan Brown. Not only did the judge rule in such a manner, but he took the time to pass comment on the accusations that had been strung out by the legal team of Baigent and Leigh. Their argument, the judge said, was "vague." They had altered their course during the trial, and had even based their entire argument on a "weak foundation."

As mentioned previously, this was a costly affair. As well as the publishing rights and the profits that had been mentioned in the case, the matter of the legal fees was decided by the court. It cost Baigent and Leigh over a million dollars to sue Dan Brown. As they were suing in Britain, this fee was usually given as being around £800,000. But not only did they fail to secure a verdict, they lost even more money. Dan Brown's legal team (and that of his publishers) was even more expensive. It cost £1.2 million. When the judge ordered Leigh and Baigent to pay 85% of Brown's legal fees, he hit the authors with a massive bill. As most people do in this situation, they filed for an appeal. By the time this was over, the legal costs had risen to over £3 million. This is just a small sliver of the money involved in modern day discussions of the Priory of Sion, and an example of why the subject is so fiercely contested.

The effects of the judge's ruling were not limited to claiming one side right and one side wrong. The case included a close textual comparison of the two books. Led by Judge Smith, this comparison can provide a bit of insight into the ways in which the two books were created and why the consistent element across the two — the Priory of Sion and the ideas it is said to protect — became such a controversial matter. While the story of how Baigent, Lincoln, and Leigh had written their book was very distinct (a matter we will come to shortly), a discussion of how the idea came to be seemed to convince the Judge that it wasn't plagiarism.

According to Dan Brown and his legal defence, the history of the Priory of Sion was told to him by his wife. Blythe Brown, who is regarded as an expert in art and often a pool of resources for her husband's books, had read *The Holy Blood and the Holy Grail*. As an art expert, she was more than familiar with many of the fundamental participants within the book, and discovered a new take on the ideas that she clearly found so interesting that she took the ideas to her husband. Blythe provided Dan with a basic rundown of the ideas outlined in the book, ideas which would eventually coalesce to become *The Da Vinci Code*.

Indeed, that the ideas were originally explored and outlined in *The Holy Blood and the Holy Grail* was never a matter which Dan Brown regarded as an issue. He went as far as to name one of the main characters of *The Da Vinci Code* after the authors of *The Holy Blood and the Holy Grail*. Leigh Teabing takes his first name from Richard Leigh, while his surname is an anagram of Baigent. It seems a knowing tip of the hat to anyone who might have encountered the story of the Priory of Sion before. In a book with a plot based on hidden clues in various masterpieces of art, Brown's own puzzle is fairly easy to decipher. It was never meant to be too well hidden.

But during the course of the case, Dan Brown and his publishers' legal team pointed out that the author in fact knew very little about the topic other than what his wife told him. The judge pointed out that it seemed to be of little interest to Brown just how the research of the non-fiction book was handled. Instead, Peter Smith seemed content to agree that Dan Brown had taken his wife's research and incorporated it into his book, happy to rely on his wife's proven research skills.

While this might point towards a questionable thoroughness in the historical accuracy of *The Da Vinci Code*, this seemed to slightly disagree with the comments made by Dan Brown following the trial. After the judge had delivered the verdict and awarded the case to Brown and his publishers, the author had come out to say that he felt the result was a victory for "artistic expression." It was important, he told the press that a novelist felt free to draw on any aspect of history that he so desired, without the fear of being sued by anyone else.

That leaves then us with a number of questions. Aside from the questionable importance placed on *The Da Vinci Code* as a great work of art, we are faced with the idea of just how much we can consider the ideas behind *The Holy Blood and the Holy Grail* to be considered history? As will become clear over the course of this book, the very idea of the Priory of Sion is up for debate. It is said that the order's existence can be traced back thousands of years, though some suggest that its reputation died that day in a London court room. When we are asking the question what exactly is the Priory of Sion, we must ask ourselves, how exactly are we able to truthfully describe anything as being a verifiable part of history?

Nowadays, the Priory of Sion is big business. If we look once again at *The Da Vinci Code*, we can see a book that was optioned to be turned into a film. Under the direction of Ron Howard and with Tom Hanks in the leading role, the film was successful enough that it has earned itself two sequels — *Angels and Demons* was released afterwards, while *Inferno* is set for release in 2016. But as well as the box office money the film generated, it managed to whip up the argument over the contents of the book all over again. The subject matter, it seems, is highly volatile. As we trace the history of the idea back from the three authors of *The Holy Blood and the Holy Grail*, this is the media frenzy that has steadily escalated over the years.

But why would it cause countries to ban the film? In India, for example, the film was criticized and outlawed for having cast aspersions over the divinity of Jesus Christ. Christianity is the largest religion in the world, with Catholicism its biggest denomination. Could one idea, put forward in a few books and a film have that big an impact?

Perhaps the answer lies with one of the authors of *The Holy Blood and the Holy Grail*. Of the three authors, it is the one who we have barely touched upon who can provide the entry point into the history of the Priory of Sion, the lens through which much of the ensuing story will make sense. His name is Henry Lincoln. Of all the people in this story, he is perhaps the sole reason why people in the English speaking world have heard of the Priory. He might even be the reason why you picked up this book. The difference is, his name is not familiar to the general public. But that is not to say that he is not famous, or well known.

Let's take a brief moment to look at the introduction to *The Da Vinci Code*. Before we delve into the history of Henry Lincoln, we should know that everyone who opened the bestselling work of fiction was met with a statement from the author. Before the book had even begun, before the reader starts to enter into the plot, the author has included a statement to be read. It places the book into a context. It starts with one very important word: *fact*. Throughout the book, there will be plot holes and sudden shocks. Albino monks will whip themselves and characters will double cross one another. This all takes place in the commonly accepted world of fiction. Read a novel and you are all too aware that what you are reading is not necessarily truth. That it, unless the author goes out of his way to suggest otherwise. In the case of Dan Brown, there is a statement of "fact" at the beginning of the book which informs readers about the world they will soon enter into.

"Fact," Dan Brown writes, "The Priory of Sion […] is a real organization." The author continues to mention a number of historical sources (which we will come to later) as a means of asserting his claim, but he leaves audiences in no doubt that the Priory itself exists. Alongside the works of art which are mentioned in the book, alongside the other pieces of historical fact, and alongside the more whimsically fictional elements of the plot, Brown insists to his readers that the Priory of Sion is a very real organization and one which will be hugely important in the following novel. It is this kind of appraisal and certainty that we must understand before we meet Henry Lincoln. Without Lincoln, no one would be quite so sure at all.

Even Baigent and Leigh would agree with the way in which Brown presents the preface to his novel. Though they might disagree with the author in a courtroom, the information contained within that statement seems very much in line with exactly what they outlined in their book, *The Holy Blood and the Holy Grail*. The third writer of that book, the one who was not present in court, was Henry Lincoln. Indeed, in the follow-up to their bestselling work of non-fiction, *The Messianic Legacy,* the three authors wrote that the information about the Priory of Sion that they revealed was enough to rock the "very foundations of Christianity." Just as with Dan Brown, Lincoln and his fellow writers were more than happy to assert the legitimacy of the Priory. If this was all quantifiable fact, if Lincoln and his fellow writers had poured so much hard work into their book, if the information in *The Da Vinci Code* was just all accepted truths, then why was the Catholic Church so angry about Dan Brown's book? Why did the whole world not know about the Priory of Sion? And where had the three authors found this hidden information?

Even though he was not present in the courtroom in London, Henry Lincoln was the point of origin for the knowledge of the Priory of Sion that we have today. As one of the co-authors of *The Holy Blood and the Holy Grail*, you might have expected to see him alongside Baigent and Leigh. But Henry Lincoln was never exactly what he seemed. To some people — and especially during the 1980s — he was better known as a television personality. He appeared on the occasional broadcast, covering history and presenting informative shows. Every now and then he would write something approaching serious material. Genial, laid back, and approachable, he was different to the stuffy television historians that had preceded him. Dressed in turtleneck sweatshirts and with a loose goatee on his face, he faced a number of enquires and discoveries with a relaxed yet plausible dignity. For a certain generation of television viewers, he was a marked break from the past and a fascinating figure in the world of televisual history.

This was not the whole truth about Henry Lincoln, however. When delving deeper into his life, we find many things that are not quite as they appear. Firstly, his real name was Henry Soskin. Many people in the entertainment industry change their names before they become famous. But what is interesting is that Henry Lincoln (or Soskin) was never actually a historian. Instead, he was an actor and a writer, and had been in the television industry for a long time. As a writer, he had worked on a number of science fiction shows, including the famous BBC series *Doctor Who*. Those who go looking for his name will find it in the credits of a 1968 film starring Boris Karloff called *The Curse of the Crimson Altar*. Henry Lincoln was a co-writer of the film. As an actor and a writer, we can take it as a given that he knew how to tell a story.

But Henry Lincoln's best story would be told time and time again, to increasingly more important people. It began with a holiday. In 1969, he recounted in the preface to *The Holy Blood and the Holy Grail*, he was on his way to the south of France. Along the way, he decided that he would buy a book. He went off searching for a paperback — something light to read on holiday — and bought a novel called *The Accursed Treasure*. The book was written in French, authored by a man named Gerard de Sede. As recalled by Lincoln, it was "lightweight" and "entertaining." It managed, he said, to blend together elements of historical fact and "genuine mystery" with just a dash of conjecture. The plot revolved around a priest in a small town in 19th century France. The priest lived in Rennes-le-Chateau, a relatively poor part of Languedoc, with a relatively poor church. But one day, the book supposed, he found an incredible secret inside his church. The secret was enough to turn the priest into a very wealthy man and his church benefitted massively.

The Accursed Treasure stuck with Henry Lincoln. Whereas the majority of people might read it once and forget about it, something about the story of the poor priest striking it lucky stayed with him. But there was a problem. While the book said that the discovery the priest had made involved "cryptic documents," the book didn't mention exactly what these documents were. These documents were even printed in the novel itself, but the author didn't provide a decryption. There were two real documents that were supposedly recovered from the church that made it into the printed book, though it was impossible to say exactly what they meant. They needed to be deciphered, a fact which clung to the inside of Henry Lincoln's skull like a limpet.

Armed with the two mysterious documents that he found in the book, Henry Lincoln set about trying to work out their hidden meaning. After not too long, he even managed it. But it was not enough. If it was this easy for Lincoln and he only had two pages from the mysterious find, why exactly had Gerard de Sede not deciphered the notes himself? For Lincoln, this simply added to the mystery. After having cracked the mystery behind the first two sheets, Henry found himself increasingly obsessed with the story. Not only did he need to decipher the rest of the papers, but he needed to let more people know about the strange documents and the message they contained. As he began to delve deeper and deeper, new secrets and "layers of meaning" began to reveal themselves to the author.

Armed with a number of these glimpses into a hidden world, Henry Lincoln set about spreading his message. He worked in the television industry already, so it seemed obvious that he should go directly to the biggest power within his business — the BBC. The British Broadcasting Corporation produced a large number of historical and documentary programs. Indeed, they even had a regular series that focused on such issues. It was called *Chronicle*. Despite the fact that Henry Lincoln was neither an academic historian nor a qualified anthropologist, the BBC decided the story was good enough to tell anyway. They commissioned Henry to produce an item to be shown on an episode of

Chronicle, which, when you consider the man's lack of qualifications, is somewhat remarkable. It is perhaps even more remarkable that Lincoln managed to convince the television executives despite being armed with nothing more than two photocopied pages taken from an obscure French paperback.

As remarkable as it might have seemed, Henry Lincoln received his funding and packed up and went off to France. An interview with Gerard de Sede was arranged. The author of *The Accursed Treasure* was set to meet Lincoln in Paris in the latter months of 1970. Though the interview was seemingly a laid back affair, Lincoln could not help himself but insistently question de Sede as to why he had not bothered to provide full deciphers for the entire text. After being badgered seemingly into submission, the Frenchman answered in a way that Lincoln remembered for the rest of his life. The decryptions had not been given, de Sede exclaimed, simply because "we thought it might interest someone like you to find it for yourself."

The French author could not have been more right. Lincoln, he could tell, was already hooked. The possibility of uncovering further information was like a drug and the British man had been given a taste. De Sede began to supply small morsels of information, drip feeding the truth behind the little church in the small town. This first code was not the only one that needed breaking, it seemed. Lincoln plunged deeper and deeper into the rabbit hole. One of the first mysteries presented to him involved the French painter Poussin. According to the author of *The Accursed Treasure*, there was a tomb hidden away in the French countryside that bore a remarkable resemblance to the one found in Poussin's painting, *Shepherds of Arcadia*. It was to be found near the church in Rennes-le-Chateau, in a place called Pontils. De Sede even had photographs. When he showed Lincoln, the similarity was both obvious and striking. Lincoln began to believe that he was on to something far bigger than just a regional legend. What he described as a "small local mystery" was beginning to take on "unexpected dimensions."

These unexpected dimensions meant that eventually there would be three entries in the *Chronicle* series. Not content with just the one short piece, Lincoln helped to produce another two on the subject of the church at Rennes-le-Chateau. The first was titled the *Lost Treasure of Jerusalem* and was aired in 1972. After a positive reception, it was followed up with 1974's *The Priest, the Painter and the Devil*. These first two entries struck a chord with the British television public. Just like de Sede's book, there was a delightful combination of codes to unravel, mysteries to be solved, secret histories, buried treasures, and a fascinating prospect. According to the films, the keys to unraveling the mysteries were hidden in pieces of art. Solve the puzzle in the art, and you would help solve the mystery. Just like the tomb in the Poussin painting, the church's secrets were seemingly known to artists.

One notable absence from the show was any form of criticism, especially from the more serious end of the historian spectrum. Airing on the BBC, one might expect the show to adhere to a certain set of standards. But no one wrote in to complain about the slacking historicism of the pieces by Lincoln. As only short segments which were appreciated by the majority, perhaps no one viewed them as being altogether too important. Not worth working a fuss up over. In an age when clumsy video recorders and no internet meant that once something was broadcast, repeat viewings were not very easy, there was little point in getting worked up over an item shown on *Chronicle*. Neither historians nor the Catholic Church felt the need to respond to Lincoln's findings.

Following the broadcast of the second entry in the *Chronicle* series, Henry Lincoln found his team was expanding. For the first time, he was working alongside Michael Baigent and Richard Leigh. Richard Leigh had been the first to enter into Lincoln's world. The two had been giving lectures at a summer school for writing in 1975. During a period of down time, they found themselves chatting about the Knights Templar and other mysteries. The subject turned to the films Lincoln was still shooting and Leigh offered his services should the man need anything clarified on the matter of the Templars. In addition, Leigh provided the introduction to Baigent, a psychology graduate who had given up a fairly profitable career working as a photographer for a news agency in order to pursue his interest in everything to do with the Knights Templar.

The trio collaborated for the first time on what would eventually become the third entry in Lincoln's series of films for *Chronicle*. This one was titled *The Shadow of the Templars* and was broadcast in 1979. In Leigh's own words, the trilogy of short films were regarded by the BBC as being the "most successful documentaries [the BBC] had ever done." More significantly, the work the trio had put into the final entry in the series had given them information that would supposedly clarify the entire mystery of the church in Rennes-le-Chateau. The work they conducted together on the short film for *Chronicle* would go on to become the foundation of *The Holy Blood and the Holy Grail*.

Anyone who has managed to catch the first entry in Lincoln's series for the BBC might remember the final words in the program. As he reminds readers in his preface to *The Holy Blood and the Holy Grail*, Lincoln was certain that "something extraordinary was waiting to be found" in the church. The book the three men wrote together hoped to uncover exactly what that extraordinary something was. By the time the book was released, people were just as curious. So much so, in fact, that on the first day of release the book sold 43,000 copies.

Despite having no real background in history, and despite taking his lead from a forgotten piece of French fanciful writing, Henry Lincoln had put into place the pieces that would transform into our modern comprehension of the Priory of Sion. It is safe to say that had Lincoln decided against taking a holiday to the south of France, the Priory might never have become public knowledge. But with so many claims being made as to the earth shattering revelations that were uncovered at the church in Rennes-le-Chateau, it might be time to examine exactly why *The Holy Blood and the Holy Grail* became such a best seller.

The Secrets of The Holy Blood and the Holy Grail

Throughout this book, we have referred time and time again to *The Holy Blood and the Holy Grail* without spending much time focusing on exactly what the books tries to accomplish. The Priory of Sion is forever bound to this book, and no explanation about the Priory and their function would be complete without first exploring a number of the ideas that are laid out by Henry Lincoln, Michael Baigent, and Richard Leigh.

There is a central thesis to the book which will be known to anyone who has read *The Da Vinci Code*. It has been mentioned several times already in this book, but let us take a brief moment to discuss the theory in full.

Put simply, *The Holy Blood and the Holy Grail* suggests that there is a secret society known as the Priory of Sion. The Priory can trace its history back to 1099, and has been led at various points by a collection of illustrious and well-known figures, each of whom inherits the title of Grand Master. It's said that previous Grand Masters have included Leonardo Da Vinci and Isaac Newton, and that the purpose of this secret society is to reinstate the Merovingian dynasty to the French throne, as well as to spread the power of the Merovingian family across Europe. The Priory believes that the Merovingian line is sacred and possesses a world-changing secret.

It is also suggested by the book that other societies — in particular, the Knights Templar — owe their very existence to the Priory's work. It is alleged that the Templars were established during the Crusades as a kind of military and financial division of the Priory of Sion. Through the Templars, the Priory could project a form of power without having to reveal themselves or place their secret in jeopardy. This secret is also the underlying hypothesis of *The Holy Blood and the Holy Grail*.

It is claimed that Jesus Christ, the founder of Christianity (and a major figure in a number of other major religions) was wed to Mary Magdalene. Not only this, but the marriage produced a number of children. From these children, it is possible to trace the bloodline of Jesus Christ from his death all the way into the modern day. Following the arrest and execution of Jesus Christ, the authors believe that Mary Magdalene and her children flew the Near East and settled in southern France. There, they intermarried with a number of important noble families. This eventually led to the rise of the Merovingian kings. The Priory of Sion believes that this bloodline should be protected at all costs.

Linked to this is the idea of the Holy Grail. A long standing item of importance in Western Christendom, the Holy Grail has been described variously as a cup or chalice that — when drunk from— can give everlasting life. It has featured in film and literature, from medieval French poetry to the Indiana Jones film franchise. However, the authors of *The Holy Blood and the Holy Grail* suggest that the Holy Grail is not a physical cup. Instead, it is a reference to two things. Firstly, to the womb of Mary Magdalene, which bore the children of Jesus. Secondly, to the bloodline of Jesus's descendants. As we will see shortly, they believe that an error in passing along the story changed the nature of the grail from this metaphysical reference into an actual physical item. Thus, the pursuit of the Holy Grail is actually a pursuit of the truth about the lineage of Jesus Christ. According to the book, his descendants still walk the earth today.

These theories were not simply plucked out of the air. During the course of their research, Lincoln and his fellow writers had come across the *Dossiers Secrets*, a collection of apparently ancient documents that were found hidden away in the National Library of France. These documents supposedly provided the authors with a detailed history of the Merovingian line. They combined this with their knowledge of the Roman Catholic Church, as well as their knowledge of history and the work they had already done in Rennes-le-Chateau. Not only did they believe that the dynasties outlined in *the Dossiers Secrets* demonstrated how the blood line traveled all the way back to Mary Magdalene, but they believed that they could use this information to show that the lineage could be traced back to King David.

In *The Holy Blood and the Holy Grail*, the Priory of Sion exists in tandem with this truth about the children of Jesus Christ. It is the job of the Priory to protect and to help the lineage. But who would they need protecting from? According to the book, it is once again the Catholic Church which takes on the role of the bad guy. In the text, the authors outline how they believe the Catholic Church has threatened the descendants of Christ. Not only have they destroyed institutions such as the Knights Templar (and the Cathars) that were set up to protect the descendants, but they have also attempted to actually kill a number of the members of the bloodline. The reason? Power.

The Catholic Church, according to *The Holy Blood and the Holy Grail*, hopes to preserve the power of the episcopal throne. That is to say, the Pope acts as the mouthpiece for God on Earth. Should a descendant of Jesus Christ himself remain alive, then it would place this power in serious jeopardy.

That leaves the Priory of Sion with a number of stated goals. The authors are able to conclude (after looking through the evidence they possess) that the Priory must be dedicated to a number of different causes, all in the name of protecting the children of Jesus Christ and Mary Magdalene.

The first of these goals is to reveal to the world the tomb of Sigebert IV and the lost treasures of the Jerusalem Temple. Both of these are supposedly the actual physical records of the genealogy of Jesus Christ. They provide apparently irrefutable proof of the fact that Jesus fathered children and that those children exist into the modern day. The tale of these items is linked to the rise of Charlemagne, the French king who overthrew the Merovingian dynasty.

The second is to promote the rise of a kind of pan-European national pride. This has been linked to the reinstitution of chivalry, the code of honorable practice known for its adoption by medieval French knights. The Priory are said to hope that the rise of chivalry will lead towards a better Europe in the future, though this is one of the claims which is most often dismissed when discussing *The Holy Blood and the Holy Grail*.

The third goal is associated with the rise in chivalric order and a pan-European sense of nationalism. The Priory hopes to see the establishment of a kind of United States of Europe, all under the banner of one religion. This Holy European Empire will be created and lead by the Merovingian (and thus holy) bloodline and will involve the conflation of both the political and religious seats of power. The Holy See will be dethroned and, in his place, the descendent of Jesus will form the spiritual and political leadership.

Finally, the authors of the book believed that — once these goals were accomplished— the Priory of Sion would be able to take on the role of a government that spans Europe. This would include the formation of a one-party government which would provide the Priory with the only means of real power.

The further one moves away from the central tenet of the book, the more it descends into the realm of typical conspiratorial notions. While there had been previous suggestions of the existence of Christ's children (and that they had been born from Mary Magdalene), *The Holy Blood and the Holy Grail* had been the first work to combine these notions with similarly far-reaching ideas of European power struggles.

This is perhaps because the authors incorporated a well known conspiratorial document into their research. Known as *The Protocols of the Elders of Zion*, the tract is distrustful of both the Masons and the Jews. As such, it has been described as both anti-Semitic and anti-Masonic. For Lincoln and his fellow writers, the ideas outlined in the document seemed to run parallel to those they were uncovering in their research into the history of the Priory of Sion. They even went a step further. According to the text, *The Protocols of the Elders of Zion* was the most damning piece of evidence for the Priory's activities. They believed that the original text (the one which had formed the basis of *The Protocols of the Elders of Zion*) had not actually had anything to do with Judaism, but had instead been issued by the Masons (specifically, those who practiced the Scottish Rite) and the inclusion of the word 'Zion' was less a reference to Judaism (as it was interpreted) but was a reference to the Priory of Sion. It was the Priory whom the Masons believed to be behind a global conspiracy, not the Jewish people.

Baigent, Lincoln, and Leigh seemed to be convinced that *The Protocols of the Elders of Zion* was not intended to be released to the public. Instead, it merely outlined the way in which the authors and their readers could wrestle control of the Freemasons in order to undermine and re-organize the church and the state. The change in the direction of *The Protocols* was made following a failed mission to attain influence in the Russian court, when Serge Nilus altered the text and released it in 1903 in order to discredit the Catholic Church. The men surrounding the Pope, it seemed to claim, were actually Jewish and Masonic conspirators, placed into positions of power. By overlooking the esoteric Christian principles so close to the Priory of Sion, Nilus managed to distance the text from the original purpose and left people down the centuries with a warped perception of the original meaning. Once again, the authors seem to suggest, the Priory of Sion faded purposefully into the background.

All of this is laid out in nearly 500 pages of text, backed up by a further 36 pages of footnotes and comments, 24 pages of pictures and photographs, as well as a 13-page bibliography which lists texts in English, German, and French. Even if the cover of the book might make it look like a thriller, the interior clearly has its sights set on academic credibility and goes to great lengths to lay out the truth of the claims. But there's a populism to the text that is not usually present in many academic works. Take for example, the way in which the story is told.

Jesus and Mary Magdalene are described as lovers. This, it is claimed, is backed up by ancient scrolls (though, in actual fact, they are books) which were discovered in Egypt in 1945 and have become known as the Gnostic Gospels. But they say the relationship between Jesus and Mary was not without its problems. The authors claim that Peter — disciple of Jesus and the man who would eventually found the Catholic Church and become the first Pope — was jealous. He did not like the intimacy displayed between the two. When Jesus was crucified, Mary fled across the water and went into hiding with her children. They are sheltered by the local Jewish community in the south of France. Already, the story is starting to feel like a drama, rather than a dry academic work.

The story picks up some four hundred years later, as the Merovingian line begins to rise to power. The French kings are eventually displaced by the Carolingians and Charlemagne and the bloodline of the Messiah is once again forced to go into hiding. From there, the descendants of Jesus transform into the French aristocrats, the House of Lorraine. When one of their members, Godfrey de Bouillon, joins the first Crusade, he is eventually awarded the crown of the conquered Holy Lands. He becomes the first Christian King of Jerusalem for hundreds of years (if ever). But the unseen hand that has been guiding his rise to the top is none other than the Priory of Sion. The secret society have yet to be named, but following the coronation, they begin to build a small priory on Mount Zion in the captured city. It lends them their name: the Priory of Sion. As they work to form the Knights Templar, they begin to excavate Solomon's Temple and discover a hidden treasure buried beneath the ancient floor. It might be the remains of Jesus Christ or the Ark of the Covenant. It could even be the documents which finally prove the existence of Christ's descendants.

The Priory remain a powerful (though hidden) force to be reckoned with for hundreds of years. It is not until 1307 that the Catholic Church finally makes a move to have them eradicated. As the French monarchy (worried about the existence of a Merovingian bloodline) and the Catholic Church (worried about potential threats to their domination of religious law) conspire against the Priory, they make a move against the public bodies. The Knights Templar is disbanded, its members rounded up and tortured. The Templars, the Church claims, are devil-worshipping usurers. Without their great banking and military organizations, the Priory of Sion flees from public sight. They have their most important secret — the truth about Jesus Christ — and they resolve to protect it at all costs.

One of the most tantalizing aspects of the book, however, is the way in which it claims that clues and hints as to the truth about the Priory have been left in many pieces of art scattered across Europe. In the hundreds of years since the Knights Templar were first prosecuted, the Priory has satisfied itself with leaving many clues about the truth in medieval and Renaissance paintings, sculptures, and tapestries. Perhaps most famous of these is the story of the Grail itself. According to the book (and in a legend that lends the work its title), the phrase which we know today as Holy Grail (San Graal) does indeed mean cup of tradition. This is where the image of the cup that bestows immortality came from. It was even said to be the cup that Jesus drank from at the last supper. But, the authors claim, this is actually a mistranslation of the truth. In reality, San Graal is Sang Real. A letter shifts from the end of one word to the next, there is a slight difference in spelling. Easy mistakes before the advent of the printing press. And most importantly, whereas San Graal might have meant the cup of tradition, Sang Real means holy blood. The lineage of the divine. The children of Jesus Christ. A clue to this, Priory historians say, can be found in a very familiar painting. Leonardo da Vinci knew the truth about the Holy Grail, which is why his depiction of the last supper does not feature a cup placed on the table in front of Jesus Christ. Clues like these attempt to inform the world of the truth without being explicit.

So, the book suggests, this fascinating history and amazing secret are now passed down from generation to generation. Over the next 650 years, the Priory of Sion recruited the best and brightest minds of their age, all under the guidance of a series of Grand Masters. They bore the secret about Jesus and Mary Magdalene while watching over the couple's descendants. It is the list of these Grand Masters that the team of Henry Lincoln, Michael Baigent, and Richard Leigh discovered in the National Library of France, hidden inside the *Dossiers*

Secrets. The list reads like a who's who of European artistic and scientific tradition. Victor Hugo. Isaac Newton. Claude Debussy. Jean Cocteau. Robert Boyle. Leonardo da Vinci.

The presentation of these ideas in an exciting and non-academic manner makes it easy to see why *The Holy Blood and the Holy Grail* was a bestseller. The knowledge it seems to confer on its readers points at a centuries old conspiracy that totally redefines everything we think we know about European history, about the most popular religion in the world, and about the current state of geopolitics. It's a revelation and it is told almost like a thriller. It even involves the reader.

We have mentioned already that Henry Lincoln's investigations involved a painting by Nicolas Poussin. *The Shepherds of Arcadia*, it is pointed out, features a tomb. On the side of this tomb, the artist had taken the time to inscribe the words 'Et in Arcadia Ego,' a hint that Poussin knew all too well.

This habit of scattering clues across artworks seems to catch up with the Priory, however. As we know, in 1885, a priest in the small southern French town of Rennes-le-Chateau suddenly came into a huge amount of money. The priest, named Berenger Sauniere, is said to have discovered that one of the pillars in his church was in fact hollow. When he opened it up, he discovered a number of encrypted documents hidden inside. Along with help from a local bishop, he worked to break the codes and discovered a secret message:

"To Dagobert II [the last of the Merovingian Kings] king and to Sion belongs this treasure and he is there dead."

The cryptic message seemed too obscure to be relevant to anything, but Sauniere realized that it referred to the lineage of Jesus Christ. Using this information (and the other proof which he found inside the column), he was able to blackmail the Catholic Church. This provided the priest with a small fortune, money which he spent on renovating the previously poor and destitute church, and decorating it with a number of decidedly un-Christian symbols.

So, to recap, it was based on this discovery that Gerard de Sede began to write his book. From there, it was picked up and read by Henry Lincoln. Then, the BBC commissioned the production of the pieces for *Chronicle*. This put Lincoln in contact with Baigent and Leigh. This led to the discovery of the documents in the National Library of France. This, finally, led to the writing of *The Holy Blood and the Holy Grail*.

The final stage in the authors' depiction of the Priory of Sion was perhaps the most audacious. After years of conducting research and tracking down all of the individual pieces that came together to make up *The Holy Blood and the Holy Grail*, they hinted as to the identity of the extant Grand Master. The man currently heading up the Priory of Sion, they believed, was named Pierre Plantard de St Clair. Pierre, they surmised, was a direct descendent of the Merovingian line and a claimant to the French throne. Thus, he was also the living embodiment of the bloodline of Jesus Christ. The reason that this information was beginning to come to light, the book claimed, was because Plantard was on the verge of launching his political career, heading up a movement which had the power to change world politics forever. What the future held for Plantard, however, the authors could not say.

The millennia-old mystery laid out by the authors of the book leads the reader right up to the moment when they are turning the pages, holding the text in their hand. It involves the reader, brings them into the fold of an ancient conspiracy.

The Holy Blood and the Holy Grail not only outlines a revolutionary plot about the history of the Catholic Church, but it deftly brings the reader into the fold. In a clever fashion, Baigent, Leigh, and Lincoln manage to make their own quest for the truth involving to the reader. Through the very act of knowing about the Priory of Sion, the authors manage to make the reader complicit in the conspiracy. This is appealing on several levels and manages to explain why such a book would prove so popular, especially when other historical non-fiction works rarely sell in such numbers. It would eventually lead to Blythe Brown picking up a copy and passing the information on to her husband. It would eventually lead to two of the authors standing in a London courtroom, accusing a fiction writer of plagiarism. It is, no doubt, directly responsible for your interest in the Priory of Sion today. But that is not to say the book was without its critics. In the next chapter, we will begin to probe a little deeper into the complexities of the book and how it weaves pieces together. In doing so, we should begin to realize the truth about the Priory of Sion.

The Royal Bloodline

It might surprise modern readers to know that *The Holy Blood and the Holy Grail* was not immediately lambasted by critics. In this modern age of instant communication and a world wide web, such a book might be expected to cause outrage across the world, the fires fuelled by the easy availability of information. In the 1980s, however, there was an excited but fairly muted response to the ideas that were put forward by the authors.

There were those who were not impressed by the concepts. Hugh Montefiore, for example, was the Anglican Bishop of Birmingham at the time of the book's release, and he went on the television to discuss the book. Also present on the show were the authors themselves. The two parties had something of a showdown about the truth behind the book, though aired as it was on late night television and involving a British priest and a group of authors, the discussion did not become too heated.

Elsewhere, there were positive reactions. In the newspapers of the day, literary critics seemed to enjoy the fascinating insight into a previously unknown world. The Times Educational Supplement, for example, listed it as "compulsive reading," while the Oxford Times described the book as being full of "well documented and often sinister facts." There were some dissenting opinions in the press. The Times Literary Supplement (in a separate review to their Educational cohorts) called the book "rather silly" and considered it to be "worthless." There did seem to be an acknowledgement of how challenging the ideas might be, with the Sunday

Telegraph concluding that the book would no doubt "infuriate many ecclesiastical authorities," even if it did concede that the authors might yet be proven right.

Even in America, on the other side of the Atlantic, people were taking notice of the book. Though the *Chronicle* series had not aired in the United States at the time, papers such as the Los Angeles Times reviewed the book and proclaimed that there was certainly enough inside to "challenge many traditional Christian beliefs."

Reviews such as these made a big difference to how the work was viewed. In bookshops, there is a considerable difference between those books which are located in the New Age or Spiritual section, and those which are found under the banner of history. Though *The Holy Blood and the Holy Grail* might normally be expected to be found in the former, due to the unqualified history credentials of its authors, the press surrounding the book meant that it was moved into the latter part of the book store. Being placed in the history section brought with it a certain cache and an expectation of diligent research and truthfulness from those who were browsing the shelves. For a book which seemed to be so obsessed with conspiracies and ancient mysteries, *The Holy Blood and the Holy Grail* did not receive the usual scepticism given to books about alien abductions or the lost city of Atlantis. It was considered a serious historical investigation, and thus the existence of the Priory of Sion was taken to be rooted in clear, well-researched historical fact. Accordingly, it sold tens of thousands of copies.

Buoyed by the success of *The Holy Blood and the Holy Grail*, the authors embarked upon not just one, but a vast number of successors across a variety of media. We have already mentioned *The Messianic Legacy* (the book's sequel) which was released less than three years later, but there were also many others, written by all three authors or individually. These had titles such as *The Dead Sea Scrolls Deception* and *The Elixir and the Stone*. Henry Lincoln took a special interest in the church at Rennes-le-Chateau and began to produce guides, videos, maps, lectures, and a library of other materials focused on the building.

In the wake of the popularity of *The Holy Blood and the Holy Grail*, there has been a tidal wave of merchandise and media focused on similar themes to the original book. It's not even limited to the original three writers. Simply typing Mary Magdalene into an internet search engine will equip you with hundreds of sources proclaiming to know the truth about the biblical figure. This is true of the Holy Grail, the Knights Templar, and many other figures that are tangentially related to the Priory of Sion. In short, it has become a booming industry.

What's more, those who have found success in publishing books on these subjects have discovered the possibility of riches and sales figures above and beyond anything normal historians might expect. It's not just books, but DVDs, CD-ROMs, and now YouTube videos that all form a new canon of Priory-related media that can almost guarantee a return on your investment. And it can all be traced back to the initial success of *The Holy Blood and the Holy Grail*. Ironically, a book which is obsessed with tracing the lineage of an important historical figure can have its influence traced over the course of almost forty years. Even this book you are reading right now is in some way related to the successes experienced by Baigent, Leigh, and Lincoln. And this is without even mentioning the astronomical success of *The Da Vinci Code*.

But all of this success brought with it an added sense of judgement. Richard Leigh and Michael Baigent were not historians, neither was Henry Lincoln (though he did play one on TV). And so, following on from the astronomical sales figures and the growing interest in the Priory of Sion and the ideas laid out in *The Holy Blood and the Holy Grail*, it should be only logical that the academic credentials of the writers would come to be questioned. When this happened, a new avenue of criticism would open. Once people started to take a critical look at the ideas behind the book, would it be able to hold up? Was the research done into the book enough to guarantee the existence of the Priory exactly as they had described?

For those who had viewed the *Chronicle* series on television or for those who had picked up *The Holy Blood and the Holy Grail* from the history section in the bookstore, there was an assumption of the rigor that had been put into the research by Henry Lincoln and his cohorts. It is a basic social contract, to presume that when a piece of media is presented in this style that it adheres to the principles of academic history. Other items featured on *Chronicle* were written and shot by qualified historians. The other books on the shelf in the store would have been written by similarly qualified people. For all intents and purposes, this wave of new media presented the Priory of Sion as part of the same canon of historical research that one might expect. It just happened to be more exciting that the typical fare, and presented like a fictitious thriller.

But while it might have been assumed that the three authors of the historical work had just lucked upon a fascinating tale during their normal courses of investigation, it became apparent that the three men were particularly interested in, shall we say, non-orthodox views of Christianity. The areas which they considered — the early days of the Church, the writing of the Bible, Freemasonry, alchemy, Renaissance art, myths, legends, and secret societies — were certainly beyond the normal bounds of historical investigation. But if it were to be assumed that the writers were adhering to traditional research principles, then there was nothing wrong with this. If anything, they should be applauded for making history so interesting and relevant to the mainstream.

But therein lay the problem. The three authors of *The Holy Blood and the Holy Grail* did not hold themselves to the accepted standards. They knew what was required of researchers in the field of history and they ignored those rules. It states as much in their book. But rather than shying away from such accusations, the trio embraced their lack of historicism. As well as having discovered the truth about the Priory of Sion and the truth about the Holy Grail, it seemed that the three men believed that they had also discovered a brand new way in which to look at history.

One need only look at some of the less exhilarating passages of *The Holy Blood and the Holy Grail*. While there are passages of the text which discuss secret societies and plots within the Catholic Church, there are also sections which are not nearly as exciting. The reader might be forgiven for glancing over the parts of the text where the authors take a moment to discuss the "sorely inadequate" techniques that they believe mark "academic scholarship." Indeed, in the next sentence, they outline their belief that they were compelled to abandon such "conventional analysis" if they were to find the "requisite connections" that exist between the "radically diverse bodies of subject matter" that they choose to investigate. That is to say, they did not believe they were required to check their research to academic standards, simply because of the subject matter that they were discussing.

As we will see later in the text, this is an incredibly significant admission, and one which will define the way in which we view the Priory of Sion, and how the group is seen by the world. It might also hold the clue as to just how a text was able to become so incredibly popular when compared to other works within the discipline. Indeed, a quick scan of the paragraph from which the above quotes were taken would serve only to furnish the reader with a number of key words. These could be "academic," "conventional," or "scholarship," all of which would hint at a higher level of academic credentials than were actually being used. By the time the full meaning behind the paragraph is clear, the less attentive reader has already moved on to exciting tales of Catholic conspiracies.

The justification given for the lack of scholarly principles in the research is said to be the subject matter itself. Since the Priory of Sion was counter to the conventional historical narrative, the writers suggests, their research should not have to adhere to the conventional standards by which historical narratives are judged. There was very little recognized previous material for them to actually study, because they were breaking new ground. The authors manage to paint a picture in the minds of the readers that their version of events is dangerous, revolutionary. Any criticism of the ideas which stemmed from the old guard, from the traditionally academic, would be obvious. It's almost like a conspiracy. Simply by pointing out the lack of standards for the research, the critics are placed firmly on the side of the bad guys. It made any criticism of the book very difficult indeed. For the authors of *The Holy Blood and the Holy Grail*, the novelist is freer than the historian. While the historian is confined and constrained by the academic rigors, the novelist can speculate, can envision, and can chase down even the slightest of leads. It made Baigent, Leigh, and Lincoln into something like detectives, adventurous men sailing dangerous seas in order to bring home the truth. It made future accusations leveled against Dan Brown all the stranger. But it was exactly this atmosphere and this approach which allowed the writers to put forward their concepts while remaining relatively free of criticism.

So what does this mean for the book? And more importantly, what does it mean for the theories the book puts forward? A close reading of *The Holy Blood and the Holy Grail* will mean that you frequently encounter words such as "if" and "probable." Turn to any random section of the book and the prose style will inevitably continue in this way. Once it has been pointed out, it is impossible to dissuade this from the mind. It is worth remembering that Lincoln and Leigh both had an extensive history in fiction writing. Their styles were far from academic.

Accomplished writers, they would know how to present an idea in the right fashion. Through their careful use of language, as authors they could write in what is best described as a presumptuous style. Leaps of faith are made, as well as assumptions. But the clever writing disguises this on first glance.

These assumptions seem, on the surface, to be perfectly reasonable. For example, Henry Lincoln asks the reader to consider two concepts. First, that a man was born of a virgin, was able to walk on the surface of water, and — after he was executed — rose from the dead. Secondly, that a man was born, got married, and raised a family with his wife. Which scenario is more reasonable, Lincoln asks the reader, which was more likely to be true? Once the reader seems to naturally assume the latter might be more reasonable, that it is the far more probably to have happened, Lincoln then uses this as a means of backing up his argument.

But this is a flawed approach. Take, for example, the gospels. In these books of the Bible, the reader is presented with the story of a man who was born of a virgin, who did walk on water, and who did come back to life. As questionable a premise as these ideas may be, they are at least mentioned in the key text of the Christian faith. The ideas put forward by Lincoln — that Jesus got married and had children — are not. They are not mentioned anywhere. The reader is not provided with any source — at least, any source that is readily available — that indicates that Jesus might have had children. Instead, the evidence put forward by Lincoln asks the reader to make an assumption. As credible as this plea might be, it is devoid of the standards that are normally required for an assertion in a history book.

Indeed, talking many years later, Henry Lincoln tells a story about how he and his fellow writers came to the idea that the bloodline of Jesus might have been linked to the Merovingian kings. Whereas a historian might have followed a series of clues within a number of texts, the story Lincoln tells seems more like the writing department of an American television show. As the writers are sat around discussing the matter, Lincoln remembers it being as though a penny suddenly dropped. Almost out of the blue, as the team were discussing how they believed there was something 'fishy' about the Merovingian line, the pieces of information all aligned. Merovingian kings. Fishy. Fish are associated with the early Christians. They were a symbol of Jesus. Fish. Jesus. Merovingian. They must all be linked. After that, Lincoln suggests, it was just a case of putting all of the pieces into place. With historical research conducted in this manner, it is easy to see why *The Holy Blood and the Holy Grail* eventually drew criticism for the way it was written.

So, where does this leave us? We can consider *The Holy Blood and the Holy Grail* as the key turning point in the story of the Priory of Sion and how its existence became known to the public. But we also know that the way in which the book was researched was not entirely in line with the standards we might expect of non-fiction history books which make far-reaching and world changing claims. If nothing else, it increases the amount of scrutiny which we should place on the authors. But should it affect the way in which we view the Priory of Sion itself? Even if the authors were pushing the envelope in terms of their research, do we need to critically examine the society itself? In the next chapter, we will begin to pick apart the story of the Priory of Sion and how it has impacted the world.

A Growing Revolt

While the initial reviews (and the sales figures) for *The Holy Blood and the Holy Grail* were good, it was not long before one or two people began to notice the cracks in the theories. Those who had paid more attention during the course of reading the book or those who already had a background in the subject matter (or even those who knew how academic research is typically carried out) began to voice their concerns over the idea that Baigent, Lincoln, and Leigh had put together. The list of criticisms began to grow and grow. Many of the comments were relatively minor, but added together to form a kind of snowball effect. As the criticisms piled up, the authors were forced to defend themselves and to defend the existence of the Priory of Sion.

If we are to look at some of the most fundamental flaws in the book's reasoning, then it might help to start at the most obvious point: the central thesis. This is the idea that the bloodline of Jesus Christ was preserved in the Merovingian monarchy and their descendants. This very idea, though seemingly possible, is limited in scope by its very nature. One major problem is the time span between the rise of the French dynasty in question and the supposed date on which Jesus Christ was executed. There are roughly four hundred years between the two events, allowing enough time for perhaps twelve or thirteen generations to have lived, died, and passed on their genetic legacy. If we are to reason in the way of the book's authors, is it not probable that these subsequent generations gave birth to more than one child each time? Is it not probably that – rather than a single, definitive bloodline – there is a sprawling family tree? If these ideas are taken to be true, there would not only be the single Merovingian dynasty, but hundreds (if not thousands) of potential descendants of Christ. If this were true, then our modern age would be filled with people who (perhaps unwittingly) were all part of the same shared ancestry. The number of potential progenies of Jesus might by now number in the millions. It would seem strange that the Priory of Sion would exist to guard only a single member of such a potentially massive family, and unthinkable that such a secret organization could keep tabs on every possible descendant.

One need only look at the royal houses of Europe for proof of this idea in practice. Queen Elizabeth II of England, for example, can trace her family roots back many centuries. Even with the huge amounts of inbreeding and intermarrying that used to define the blue bloods of the Old World, the current Queen of England shares her ancestry with many thousands of others. Not all of them are considered royalty. But with the coups, wars, successions, revolutions, and abdications that have occurred throughout European history, there is always potentially someone who is primed to take over. The idea that there might be one single living descendant of Jesus Christ (who is guarded by the Priory of Sion) seems almost ridiculous when stepping back from the book for a moment.

Which brings us neatly to Pierre Plantard. Plantard occupies a unique role in this story, in that *The Holy Blood and the Holy Grail* specifically names him as the living successor to Jesus Christ. This is a huge mantle to place on any one person. That they also describe him as the extant Grand Master of the Priory of Sion adds another string to Plantard's increasingly busy bow. But what did Plantard himself believe?

Despite the claims made by the authors of the bestselling book, Pierre Plantard has never once described himself as a potential relation to Jesus Christ. While it is certainly true that he believes he can trace his lineage back to Dagobert II (the last of the Merovingian kings), he has distanced himself from the claims made about his family, which were mentioned in *The Holy Blood and the Holy Grail*. Indeed, by 1983, Plantard was specifically going out of his way to deny the theories put forward in the book and to disavow himself of any knowledge or station that the authors might have thrust upon him.

Another major point of contention raised by the book's critics concerns the actual idea of the Holy Grail itself. This concept, when looking back through the history books, does not appear to have existed before the twelfth century. As it stands, many researchers into medieval French literature have credited Chretien de Troyes with having invented the idea. The French poet worked under the patronage of Count Philip, ruler of Flanders, and was an author of knightly romances. These chivalric tales were immensely popular during the time and one of them — The Story of the Grail — proved to be a hugely successful poem. As with all successful poems of the day, it was borrowed, copied, reworked, and retold extensively. Historian Richard Barber has gone as far as to say that, prior to 1180, no one would have had any clue as to what exactly a Holy Grail might have been at all. By extension, Barber comments that the 'Sang Real' reasoning given in *The Holy Blood and the Holy Grail* is nothing more than an error deriving from the mistranslation by an English writer of the original French text that was made in the 15th century. Far from conclusive proof, the mistake seems to have been a genuine product of an age before the printing press, when all book production was done by hand.

Even the story of the priest that is so central to Henry Lincoln's retelling is questionable. Berenger Sauniere, the head priest of the church at Rennes-le-Chateau, was said to have mysteriously come into a huge amount of wealth, a phenomena which the book attributes to his uncovering the truth about the lineage of Jesus and the Priory of Sion's secret. But we have the records for Sauniere's church. While he did fund renovations for the building, we know that this was accomplished through the selling of masses, a popular means of fundraising for a church at the time. From 1896 up until 1905, the priest advertised the sale of his masses in the local newspapers. Clients could pay via postal order and would receive a mention during the church service (a boon when they eventually ascended to heaven and stood to be judged before the pearly gates.) The venture was so successful that the priest was receiving as many as 150 postal orders a day, order which came not just from small religious communities, but from people outside of France. Even despite this success, Sauniere himself was far from rich. There are records of the priest applying for a bank loan in 1913, with the paperwork placing his personal finances at just thirteen thousand francs. If he had uncovered a secret that threatened the very foundations of the Catholic Church, he was by extension terribly unskilled in the art of blackmail.

Staying in Rennes-le-Chateau, one of the claims made in *The Holy Blood and the Holy Grail* is demonstrably false. The book suggests that Berenger Sauniere discovered that one of the pillars in the church was hollow. It even goes as far as to suggest that this particular pillar was constructed in a Visigoth style, linking it artistically to the Merovingian dynasty. Within this hollow pillar, the authors claim, the priest found a number of hidden parchments. But this pillar still exists in the church. As any visitor to the building will notice, it is far from hollow. Like every other pillar in the building, it is solid. There are no hidden compartments.

Another artistic error in *The Holy Blood and the Holy Grail* involves the tomb supposedly depicted in the work of French artist Poussin. Lincoln recollects how he was informed during his investigation that the tomb bore a striking resemblance to a real life counterpart. This much is true. Which tomb was the original, however, was a fact that Lincoln got drastically wrong. The tomb, which is near Rennes, that Lincoln was pointed towards was not centuries old. It had been constructed in 1903 and belonged to the wife of a local land owner. Poussin's painting was completed around 250 years earlier. It is possible to comb through the text line by line and point out the numerous errors in this fashion. Pointing out these first few, however, can begin to show of just how little the research holds up under close inspection.

The Truth

But even as the story begins to unravel, it can help to pay an increased amount of attention to the plight of Pierre Plantard. Unlike the other errors committed during the research of the book, Plantard was the only person who was directly named (and was alive to deal with the resulting attention.) If, as suggested in the book, Plantard was the supposed descendant of Jesus Christ, how would this affect his life? One thing that it certainly accomplished was forcing people to look closer at the man's history, something which he may or may not have desired.

One of the facts uncovered during an investigation into the supposed last in the Merovingian line related to one of the more troubled times in France's recent history. In the latter months of 1940, France found herself occupied by Nazi Germany. The invaders sought to set up a government in France, one which they controlled and through which they could rule over the country. This was known as the Vichy government, due to the location of its headquarters, and was headed up by a man named Marshal Petain. One day, Petain received a letter from a man signing his name as Varran de Varestra. The message was a plea, with the writer begging Petain to involve France in no further combat. Rather than asking for an end to the conflict, however, the author of the letter specifically cited "Masonic and Jewish" conspirators as posing a direct threat to France and even the world. The writer of the letter claimed to have "about a hundred reliable men" on his side who were "devoted to our cause." If Marshal Petain gave the order,

Varran de Varestra and his reliable men who would leap to defeat the conspiracy.

The letter seemed to cause something of a stir within the halls of the Vichy government. An investigation was conducted and a report was put together at the request if the Secretary of State for the Interior. According to the findings, this so-called 'Varran de Varestra' was none other than Pierre Athanase Marie Plantard, who had been born in Paris on the 18th of March, 1920. He was described as a bachelor and the son of French parents, one of whom was a butler who had died in a work accident. At the time the letter was written, Plantard was living with his mother in a two bedroom apartment, surviving on the money from his mother's pension.

Pierre Plantard, it seemed, had a long history in a number of organizations. He had established and maintained a number of groups, many of whom had a decidedly anti-Semitic and anti-Masonic tilt. La Renovation Nationale Francaise, Plantard's then-current group, was described by the officer who conducted the investigation as being "purely a figment of the imagination of Plantard." While the group's leader claimed that there were 3,245 members, there were in fact only four. The report went on to describe Plantard as being "one of those dotty, pretentious young men" who set up and ran fictitious groups such as these "in an effort to look important." The report was damning.

So Plantard dropped off the radar for a number of years. He resurfaces in the government records in 1954, when it is reported that he was held in custody in Germany after it was revealed that he was attempting to organize the meeting of a secret society. The post-war government in Germany did not approve of such things and thus held Plantard before realizing he posed little threat to anyone. He appears again in police records in 1956, this time in his native France. This time, the mayor of Annemasse — a town in Haute-Savoie where Plantard was now living — discussed the imprisonment of one Pierre Plantard in 1953, mentioning that he had been found guilty of "offences against property." But it is in 1956, in the same town of Annemasse, that we find one of the most important pieces of evidence in this entire book. During the summer of that year, a man named Pierre Plantard went to the government offices and registered a new organization. He described himself as one of four founding members, people who were tasking themselves with "the defence of the rights and freedoms of low cost housing." The name he choose for the organization was the Priory of Sion. But after this sudden introduction into the annals of government, Plantard and the Priory drop off the radar.

At this juncture, it is important to introduce another player. Noel Corbu comes to us in the first months of 1956, after a number of articles about him began to appear in the French press. At the time, we know that he was not only a restaurant owner in Rennes-le-Chateau, but was now the owner of the estate of Berenger Sauniere. His hotel, Hotel de la Tour, was located in a fairly isolated location and many saw his appearances in the papers as an attempt to drum up publicity and encourage a few more guests to come and visit. The business had been open for almost a year and it seemed that the owner's main method of advertising involved telling people about a mysterious past filled with treasure and conspiracies. One only need take a look at one of the headlines of a Corbu interview to know the angle he was trying to promote. It read 'the Billionaire Priest of Rennes-le-Chateau's Fabulous Discovery.'

We don't know the exact details of what happened next in the story, but it is clear that during the course of the next five years, Plantard traveled to meet Corbu. Plantard had learned about the story of Berenger Sauniere and his sudden fortune. It had captivated Plantard and he wanted to know more. While it might be true that he was interested in the narrative aspects of the legend, it might be more likely that he recognized the financial potential that lay within the story. For a man who dreamed of carving out a self-important niche in the world, this was an amazing opportunity. And so, after consulting with Corbu, Plantard began to write a book. It was loosely based on the story of Berenger Sauniere and the church at Rennes-le-Chateau, though it incorporated a number of key additions. Details such as the cryptic documents hidden inside the Visigoth pillar were entirely Plantard's creation. He even went so far as to have the documents themselves constructed. A man named Phillipe de Cherisey (described as a "boozy but bright aristocrat") forged the papers that were said to be taken from the church. But the group did not stop there. They also manufactured a second set of documents and placed them into the National Library of France in a covert operation. If Plantard's story were ever doubted, he had already planted the corroborating evidence.

The only problem was that Plantard was an awful writer. He had put together a book describing the mystery of Rennes-le-Chateau and passed it around to a number of publishers. But no one wanted it. So Plantard turned to another of his friends, an author named Gerard de Sede. De Sede took the book Plantard had been working on, tidied it up, and eventually had it published in 1967. When we look into the details of the publishing contract, we see some interesting additions. Philippe de Cherisey, for example, is noted as being entitled to a share in the profits. We even have a collection of letters that were sent back and forth between De Cherisey, Plantard, and De Sede which discuss how their elaborate hoax was progressing and the numerous strategies which they developed in case anyone should accuse them of lying. One such strategy was to make use of an organization Plantard had already registered, the Priory of Sion, and plant evidence of its ancient history in the National Library. It would sit there for years, undiscovered, until an inquisitive hand plucked it from the shelf and used it to prove the existence of the Priory. That inquisitive hand belonged to Henry Lincoln.

It was not long after the publication of *The Holy Blood and the Holy Grail* that all of this was revealed to the public. A journalist named Jean Luc Chaumeil, writing in 1983, was living on the fringe of the group of men who worked so hard to set up the hoax. He knew them personally and even exchanged communications. He had in his possession not only a series of letters detailing the plan, but a 44-page confession written by Philippe de Cherisey which outlines how the forgery was handled. After Chaumeil launched his accusations against the group, other researchers such as Robert Richardson, Paul Smith, and Henry Cran (a producer for the BBC) began to look into the stories of Henry Lincoln and his fellow writers. It was Cran, researching the theories put forward in the *Chronicle* films, who began an investigation into the Priory of Sion and its legitimacy. His findings formed the foundations of a 1996 episode of *Timewatch* titled the History of a Mystery, in which he managed to trace the family tree of the Plantard family back as far as the 16th Century. He discovered that, rather than dethroned royalty, Plantard's ancestor was in fact a walnut farmer.

And this is where the truth finally becomes clear. It was a hoax. A conspiracy. An attempt to trick the public. Pierre Plantard, far from being the last in the bloodline of Jesus Christ, was a chancer who had hoped to make a name for himself. He had no idea that a group of writers from England would be so easily fooled by his games, especially to the extent that they were. What had begun as a small lie — perhaps even an attempt to drum up business for a failing hotel — had turned into an international sensation. The publication of *The Holy Blood and the Holy Grail* changed everything. It brought an increased scrutiny to Plantard's story, which buckled under the weight of the investigation.

It soon became clear that the long lines of names and genealogies that had been presented as evidence were in fact simply copied from other documents. They had been tinkered with here and there, made to fit, while others were simply travelogues which had been repurposed for the situation. We even know what motivated the people to invent their stories. De Cherisey states his interest in surrealism and had a background in experimental fiction, including being a member of the 1960s organization, the Workshop for Potential Literature, which saw its members invent puzzles, codes, ciphers, and tricks on a regular basis. Plantard, as should be obvious by this point, was desperate in his quest for attention and had always seen the construction of mysterious secret societies as a means to that end. Many of the other participants — Gerard de Sede and

Noel Corbu, for example — simply hoped to make a bit of money and never expected Plantard's plan to explode in popularity as it did.

It must have been strange to see the group of men as they steadily began to feed Henry Lincoln more and more information. Lincoln seemed genuine in his intrigue, convinced in the true nature of the conspiracy he was beginning to unravel. In that respect, the French conspirators played him perfectly. They were always on hand to provide a nudge in the right direction or a hint about where to look for a clue. In many respects, they allowed Lincoln to work himself into the story, to become a part of the legacy of the Priory of Sion in much the same way that readers of *The Holy Blood and the Holy Grail* were seduced by the book. It must have been astonishing to the original plotters to discover that not only had they successfully tricked Lincoln into creating the film about their invention, but also that they managed to string him along for a further ten years, during which time he shot two more films and brought in his fellow investigators.

But by the mid-nineties, well after the release of the best-selling book, Plantard seemed unable to perpetuate his invention. By this time, his true nature had been revealed, rather than the invented persona as a descendant of Jesus Christ. This resulted in an admission — under oath in a French courtroom — that Plantard had invented everything. The entire business, he admitted, was nothing more than a fraud.

His death in 2000 was not met with revulsion or derision, as some might expect for an extravagant fraudster. Nor was he mourned as the last in a divine bloodline. Rather, his death was treated with something of a nostalgic remembrance. France had lost a jovial and mostly harmless conman. By this point in time, there was no one left to believe his story and the entire episode was seen as something of a humorous incident. Well done, people thought, at managing to trick the English writers. Very funny indeed. But while everyone in France seemed to be able to see Plantard for what he really was, there were a few people who still clung to the belief that he had been telling the truth. They still believed in the Priory of Sion. Among them were Michael Baigent, Richard Leigh, and even Dan Brown. Thanks to their continued belief, the story of the Priory of Sion is far from over.

The Victims of the Priory

As it stands, then, there is indeed a conspiracy surrounding the Priory of Sion. The only problem is that it is an entirely different conspiracy than the one we set out to investigate. At the beginning of this book, we began with the promise of uncovering a millennia-old secret that concerned the very founding principles of the world's foremost religion. But as we trace the story further and further backwards in time, it soon becomes very clear that the original premise is built on very shaky foundations. Despite the claims of truth that are reiterated throughout works such as *The Da Vinci Code* and *The Holy Blood and the Holy Grail*, we are left with a certainty that the entire affair has been an attempt to pull the wool over the public's eyes. Rather than a story that begins close to 0 BC, our story really starts around 1950 AD and tries to write itself into the history books. While we originally set out to uncover the victims of an ancient Catholic conspiracy, we should ask ourselves who became the victims of a modern attempt at fraud?

Perhaps the most obvious victim is Henry Lincoln. We can have little doubt that — at least in 1969, when Lincoln first went on holiday to the south of France — he honestly believed in the truth of the story he began to uncover. As recently as 2004, he was discussing Pierre Plantard with an interviewer. During the course of the discussion, Lincoln mentioned that the now-deceased Plantard would have made an excellent poker player. With an increasing degree of vehemence, Lincoln passes over the Frenchman's unreadable qualities and mentions that we as a public actually know very little about Pierre Plantard, much in the same way that we know very little about Berenger Sauniere. Furthermore, he exclaimed, we know very little about the Priory of Sion. In fact, he finished, we know almost nothing at all. Lincoln, during the remainder of the interview, laments the existence of "demonstrable facts," as he calls them. As he admits, the majority of writing is actually "hearsay evidence, guesswork and interpretation." As Lincoln confesses, none of the written works on the subject — including his own — hold any validity at all.

This is a damning statement. It seems to be both a confession and a ray of hope. Even if he admits to the fact that his own book contains a huge amount of speculation, the lack of provable knowledge about the background of Plantard (and the Priory of Sion) seems to be an indication that there could well be something there. If only we were to dig a little deeper or search a little harder, we might be able to finally uncover the evidence of the Priory of Sion that men such as Henry Lincoln have been searching for over many decades.

But as damning as Lincoln's interview might be, it is also untrue. It is false to say that we know nothing about Plantard or Berenger Sauniere, or even — by extension — about the Priory of Sion. In fact, we actually know quite a large amount. One of the best-known facts we have in our possession is the knowledge that the existence of the Priory of Sion is a lie. It is a scam. A con. A fraud, and one which tricked Lincoln completely. Henry Lincoln was perhaps the first major victim of this con and, so complete was the trick that the con seems to have endured to this day. At the back of Henry Lincoln's mind is an insistent suggestion that there might actually be a Priory of Sion after all. It niggles away at him and refuses to allow him to disavow the theory altogether.

So while we know that the Priory of Sion was indeed a conspiracy created by a small group of French con men, we know that the first victims were actually those who did the most to popularize the lie. That leads us to the next step in the process and one of the most important questions of all. Were the writers of *The Holy Blood and the Holy Grail* simply the victims of a hoax? Did they willingly allow themselves to be deceived? Or were they even a part of the deception themselves?

For more information on this question, it might help to turn to one of the writers who did actually expose the lies behind Plantard and the Priory of Sion. Jean Luc Chaumeil released his own book in 1979, which was only a short time after the broadcast of the last in the series of films Henry Lincoln produced for *Chronicle*. It was still a good three years before the release of the book by Henry Lincoln, Richard Leigh, and Michael Baigent, at a time in which these three men were said to be conducting their (supposedly) rigorous research. In a later interview with Channel Four television (a British broadcaster), Chaumeil mentions a story about how he tried to get in contact with the men who were writing *The Holy Blood and the Holy Grail*. Chaumeil is adamant that he attempted to contact the trio up to a year before their book was published in order to alert them to the nature of the scam.

Such an allegation would have a big impact on how we view the authors of *The Holy Blood and the Holy Grail*. Had they intentionally ignored such a warning and published their ideas anyway, at least without checking up on Chaumeil's comments, then it would render their decision making process questionable, to say the least. Such an accusation was directly leveled at Michael

Baigent himself during the filming of an investigation by the actor and television historian Tony Blackburn. When asked whether the French journalist's accusations were true, Baigent states that he cannot recall the incident. Not only this, but he goes on to state that Chaumeil was "never necessarily very close to the inner groups of the Priory." It is unclear to whom Baigent is referring in this comment. It might be a reference to the group of men who had created the Priory and forged the documents that had so successfully fooled people. Or, conversely, it might be a reference to the actual Priory of Sion themselves.

But thankfully, Tony Robinson followed up the question and asked Baigent about his opinions on Chaumeil's allegations that the entire Priory of Sion organization was nothing more than a surrealist fantasy. Baigent's answer is simple and to the point. "He's wrong," Baigent exclaims. When asked how he can be quite so sure that the journalist's version of events is incorrect, Baigent puts forward his own research skills and abilities forward as proof. He has seen the documents himself, Baigent tells his interviewer, has researched them and spent six years examining and learning about the Priory of Sion. To that extent, and with all of his research having been done, Baigent states that he is "satisfied that the Priory exists." It would be hard for Baigent to be any clearer on his views. Even in recent times, he seems convinced that the documents and histories that he presented to the world in *The Holy Blood and the Holy Grail* were entirely legitimate.

In actual fact, Baigent has gone on record time and time again and reiterated that he believes both he and his team checked, examined, and verified all the information they came across in the course of their research. Not only does Baigent claim that he and the team checked everything they could, but he was happy with their conclusion, that it "proved accurate." The style and diligence of this checking is not mentioned, however, though it cannot have been entirely thorough. By 1993, every person involved in the French side of the hoax had as much as admitted their guilt. The documents — including the *Dossiers Secrets* that had been hidden in the National Library of France — had been confirmed as fakes.

But Baigent did not relent. *The Holy Blood and the Holy Grail* was reprinted in 1996 and the author took the time to address these accusations in an afterword he wrote especially for the new edition. Along with the other authors of the book, it was argued that the accusations leveled against the book and its theories stood on shaky ground. Baigent, Leigh, and Lincoln suggested that Plantard did not stand to "gain financially or in any other way" from fabricating the documents. They reiterated once again that they believed there was no reason to doubt Plantard's word. It seems a stretch that the authors could truly believe that Leonardo da Vinci and Sir Isaac Newton had led hidden lives and kept the secret of the bloodline of Jesus Christ, but not that Pierre Plantard could have invented or lied about the Priory of Sion.

It is the origins of the Priory that have caused the loudest defences from the authors of *The Holy Blood and the Holy Grail*. In the follow up to their best-selling book, titled *The Messianic Legacy*, the authors doubled down on their belief in the existence of the Priory of Sion. Though the book was published in 1987, long after

Chaumeil's articles revealed the truth, Baigent, Leigh, and Lincoln reiterated their belief in the Priory's authenticity. Not only that, but the sequel made it clear just what they thought of the accusations that their previous claims might not have been true. In one section of the book, the authors admit that "nothing appeared straightforward" when they were researching the Priory. They enter into a vivid description of the nature of the Priory of Sion in which they compare its existence to "a holographic image." This image, they say, shifted, altered, and appeared differently under changing lights. From one side, the book claims, the Priory of Sion appeared to be an "influential, powerful and wealthy international secret society," though they concede that, in another light, the Priory might appear to be nothing more than a "dazzlingly ingenious hoax devised by a small group of individuals for obscure purposes of their own." Perhaps, the authors suggest, both views were true.

This is an interesting tactic by the writers. In writing this passage, they place their own interpretation of the hoax on equal footing with the truth. Both versions are equal, they seem to suggest, just different perspectives. But while the idea that the Priory of Sion is nothing more than a con was backed up by reams of evidence and confessions, their own claims about the true nature of the Priory was still based on documents which were known to be fraudulent. While it might seem that the authors were being reasonable in adding an element of doubt, their acquiescence is nothing of the sort. Once again, they resort to depending on poor and inadequate research skills, wrapped up in convincing rhetoric.

One need only look at Baigent's background for some insight into why he might want to believe in the Priory of Sion. The man's personal history points towards someone who could very easily fall into the belief that there might be a negative agenda hidden within the Catholic Church. As per his own recollections, Baigent was raised in a devoutly Catholic household. His entire youth featured a dedication to the church, so it's possible that any rejection of their teachings could be a form of anti-establishment resentment. In his home town in New Zealand, Michael Baigent and his family would attend their local Catholic church at least three times a week. From the age of five, he was even given private lessons from a theology tutor on the history and doctrine of the Catholic Church. Like most teenagers, he rebelled against his parents and the overarching institutions in his life. But while some teenagers turn to drink or drugs, the young Michael Baigent still felt the need to scratch a religious itch. For a period, he began to attend every different kind of church that he could. The Anglicans, the Methodists, the Presbyterians, and even the Mormons all welcomed him into their church. But he never quite found the answers he was looking for.

Later, when he went away to university, Michael Baigent changed his area of study. Though he had originally been signed up to a science degree, he decided to switch courses and take comparative religion. Perhaps if he had stayed his original course he might have gained a better understanding of how to achieve provable results through research. Nevertheless, his interests while at university began to grow increasingly esoteric. As well as his comparative religion classes, he began to stretch his interests into more obscure branches of theology. He joined a group named the Builders of

Adytum, who practiced the little understood art of Christian Kabbalah. Up until his graduation, he maintained an interest in the less mainstream aspects of the Christian world, miles away from his Roman Catholic upbringing.

Eventually, this path brought him to England. Moving to London in the 1970s, he moved into a flat with a man named Richard Leigh. The two became great friends and soon discovered a shared passion for the stranger aspects of religion. By this time, Baigent was pursuing a mildly successful career as a photojournalist. But when Richard Leigh introduced Baigent to a man named Henry Lincoln, he was quick to give this up. After Lincoln outlined his interests in the film he was currently making for the BBC, Baigent quickly sold all of his photography equipment in order to fund his research with the pair of writers. He even started working night shifts at a nearby soft drinks factory in order to pay his way while carrying out the preliminary research on what would eventually become *The Holy Blood and the Holy Grail*. It is safe to say by this point that Michael Baigent was heavily invested in the existence of the Priory of Sion and was obsessed with the possibility that there might be a hidden meaning behind the Catholic doctrine. The discoveries made by the team provided him with the ideal justification for his growing suspicions about organized religion, as well as indulging his fascination with the esoteric practices. Baigent says as much, admitting during his deposition in court that "with hindsight, I had become obsessed with [the Priory of Sion]."

Even after the release of *The Holy Blood and the Holy Grail*, Michael Baigent was seemingly still wrapped up in his obsession. A man named Paul Smith, a noted sceptic of the ideas laid out in the book, recalls going to visit Baigent in 1993. Though Smith insists that Baigent was both hospitable and courteous, he seemed surprised to note that the man remained adamant about the existence of the Priory of Sion, that the Merovingian bloodline could be easily traced to the modern age, and that the Line of David (and thus Jesus Christ) was a probable fact. Even when looking through the papers and documents that Baigent kept in the home, Smith discovered various sources that seemed to conclusively prove that the story of Sauniere and the church at Rennes-le-Chateau was a myth. Either they were ignored or dismissed. According to Smith, these notable pieces of evidence lay in the hands of someone who "did not know how to use [them] properly." Baigent, Smith says, was more interested in pursuing "non-sequiturs relating to pseudo-history."

The more we learn about Michael Baigent, the more it becomes possible to sympathise with him. Though he might well have been proven wrong time and time again, there is nothing malicious in his continued belief in the existence of the Priory of Sion. Rather, he seems to be a man who is always able to look in another direction when confronted with evidence that runs contrary to his world view. That is not to say that he does not thoroughly examine 'evidence.' During the course of the research for *The Holy Blood and the Holy Grail*, Baigent and his fellow writers examined a huge amount of information over the course of many years. The issue is the critical approach Baigent and his colleagues were able to take. Every time they evaluated a source, they seemed happy to use only information which ratified their beliefs, and dismiss anything that might dissuade them from their opinions. Confessions and conspiracies from men such as Pierre Plantard were readily dismissed because Baigent and his fellow writers approached the idea of the Priory of Sion with an almost religious fervour. They had faith in the idea, even when all evidence ran to the contrary.

There is an anecdote which can provide some insight into the matter. The one-time editor of the *Spectator*, Matthew d'Ancona recalls a lunch meeting that was held in the 1990s in a restaurant in central London, named L'Amico. The meeting was held between two distinct 'sides.' On one hand were a group of right of center political thinkers whose chief unifying ideology was that they all wanted to withdraw Britain from the European Union. On the other side were a group whom D'Ancona described as 'men who don't get out very much.' These were Michael Baigent and Richard Leigh. The meeting had been put together by the two authors with the aim of probing the Eurosceptic group for information. D'Ancona recalls the question being asked as to whether the right wingers had ever come across anything peculiar in their drive to separate Britain from the EU? Had they ever had the sensation that there might be some hidden agenda to the formation and rise of the European Union? Could it be that — rather than creating a federation of nations for the purposes of trade and governance — there might be a cover intention to accomplish something as strange as to restore the bloodline of Jesus Christ to a position of power, perhaps? According to D'Ancona, the authors of *The Holy Blood and the Holy Grail* put together the lunch meeting with the soul intention of reaffirming one of their more outlandish ideas. It speaks volumes of the lengths to which they would go to prove themselves right. It seems strange to consider this the work of men who might be acutely aware of the inherent falsity of their own ideas.

It certainly seems as though there is a legitimate belief among the writers of *The Holy Blood and the Holy Grail* that the Priory of Sion actually exists. Certainly Michael Baigent and Richard Leigh seem convinced by the evidence they have seen, to the point where they were willing to defend themselves under oath. Even the principles behind their lawsuit against Dan Brown seem to suggest that it was the suggestion that their ideas might be fallible that caused the real issue, rather than literal plagiarism. But there was one man who was absent from the trial. Trying to pin down the beliefs of Henry Lincoln seems a bit harder.

Some suspect that Henry Lincoln was much quicker to realize the truth behind the Priory story. After having worked as a writer in film and television for many years, he was well aware of what it took to tell a story and to tell it well. It might even be that once he noticed the money that was to be made from writing *The Holy Blood and the Holy Grail*, he saw it as being no different than penning another episode of *Doctor Who* or some other science fiction B movie. Lincoln was a man who had already built a television career on a slight deception. He was not a historian nor an archaeologist, though was more than happy to present himself as one on *Chronicle* and other TV shows. How was participating in the conspiracy behind the Priory of Sion any different than pretending to be an historian? Certainly, it seems, the truth was not the be all and end all for Henry Lincoln.

In the years since *The Holy Blood and the Holy Grail* was released — and especially more in the wake of *The Da Vinci Code*'s success — Henry Lincoln has given many interviews. One of these in particular gave a slight insight into the way he views the evidence for the existence of the Priory of Sion. During the course of the discussion, Lincoln quite freely admits that the documents themselves — such as the *Dossiers Secrets* — are proof of "absolutely nothing" except the fact that the documents have been created. This, he says, is true of all documents. Lincoln finishes the rather abstract thought by stating that "nothing is better than anything else."

"In history," he suggests, "nothing is real so there's nothing to get hung up about." It is a telling admission of how Lincoln views his work on the history book. It speaks of how far his standards of evidence are from the typical historian's and how he views his work as being more akin to a novel than an actual academic work. If anything, the comments of Henry Lincoln seem to place him on an equal footing to Dan Brown. Perhaps the reason why he was not present at *The Da Vinci Code* trial was that he saw too much of himself in Dan Brown. To criticize Brown would be to admit he himself was wrong. While he may have truly believed in the existence of the Priory of Sion at the time of writing, it seems that Lincoln is alone among the authors in realizing the true nature of the organization.

The Fallout

During the course of this book, it has become increasingly clear that any assertion as to the existence of the Priory of Sion is fundamentally flawed. Nevertheless, this has not stopped numerous publications — books, leaflets, articles, films, television programmes, and other media — from shouting loudly about the ideas put forth in *The Holy Blood and the Holy Grail*. Even after the fallout from the French conspiracy has proven these ideas to be false, people have taken these concepts and run with them. Today, there are myriad media sources that profess to be able to inform the audience of the reality behind the legend. Despite the evidence that has been put forth, what do people still think about the Priory of Sion today?

As might be expected, there are hundreds of competing theories as to the true nature of the Priory. A quick Google search will return over 360,000 results just for the search terms 'Priory of Sion.' There are dedicated websites, Wikipedia pages, and YouTube videos, all of which profess to give the public the best possible explanation of what the society is. As well as this, Google will make some suggestions to the avid searcher, mentioning Knights Templar, Mary Magdalen, Opus Dei, and the Illuminati as searches which are related to the Priory of Sion. It quickly becomes clear what kind of company the search terms keep.

For those who have spent a great deal of time trawling through the information that is available online, there are a number of repeated themes and ideas. As you read through web page after web page, these ideas will crop up time and time again. A number of these have not been touched on yet by the book but now seem essential to the modern interpretation of the Priory of Sion. So let us take the time to follow a few of these tangents, in order that we might better understand what the Priory of Sion means in the modern Internet age.

Mary Magdalen

Mary Magdalen is perhaps one of the most important persons in this story and one who we have barely touched upon during the course of this book. She is an important figure in the story of the Priory of Sion, and one who extends beyond the realms of the questions of fraud and delusion that mark so many of the other topics in this text. Though her name is famous around the world, there is a huge amount of misunderstanding about exactly who Mary Magdalen was, and what her role was in relation to the biblical figure of Jesus Christ. Her story is marked by vicious attacks on her character and possibly one of the earliest examples of slander and misrepresentation. But who exactly was Mary Magdalen?

Perhaps some of the confusion over the identity of Mary Magdalen comes from the fact that she shares her name with a far more famous biblical figure. Not to be confused with the woman who gave birth to Jesus — the Virgin Mary, or Mary of Bethany — who was the sister of Lazarus, she occupies a slightly strange role in the story of the New Testament. Just like the apostles, she is said to have traveled around with Jesus and is a figure in many of the stories of the biblical son of God. Chief among these is the story of his death, whereupon she witnesses the crucifixion and the resurrection up close.

Across all four gospels, her name is mentioned twelve times. Though it might seem like a low number, this is actually higher than many of the lesser known disciples.

However, during the Middle Ages, there was a distinct shift in the way in which she was presented to the world. Though the biblical sources seem to depict her as another follower of Christ, her reputation was tarred. Erroneously (according to most scholars) Mary Magdalen was presented as a "repentant prostitute" to the followers of Western Christianity. Supported by very little evidence in the actual Bible, many preachers, clerics, and members of the holy orders were more than happy to describe Mary Magdalen as something of a "loose woman." Over the ensuing centuries, she became known more for her manufactured past as a prostitute rather than her devotion to the biblical Jesus.

So, if Mary did not deserve this reputation, what does the bible actually say about her? Well, we do know that it says Jesus cast out seven demons that had been inhabiting her body. In both the gospels of Luke and Mark (the latter of which expands more on the topic), she is mentioned as a woman who followed Jesus and the apostles as they "traveled about from one town and village to another." It was Jesus, they state, who cleansed Mary of the seven demons that had beset her, which some people have interpreted as being the curing of mental health issues which were not well understood at the time.

It is during the crucifixion that Mary Magdalen plays a real role, however. During the execution of Jesus Christ, she witnesses three major events. She is present at the crucifixion itself, at the burial, and is one of the people who notices that the tomb is empty a few days later. All of Mark, Matthew, and John mention her specifically by name during these events while Luke, who mentioned no names, does recall the presence of "women who had followed [Jesus] from Galilee." As such, it is safe to assume that — in any biblical portrayal of the execution of Jesus Christ — Mary Magdalen was present.

But she also plays a far more important role. In Mark, Matthew, and John, it is Mary Magdalen who is the first witness to the most important of Christian events: the resurrection. Three of the gospels describe either Mary Magdalen alone or with others as being the first person to notice that the tomb of Christ is empty. In a number of passages from Mark and John, it is made clear that she was the first person to whom the resurrected Christ appeared. In certain passages, it is made clear that this meeting is a private one shared between Jesus and Mary Magdalen, a privilege not afforded to many of the more esteemed apostles. It seems, then, that she plays a very important role in the life of Jesus Christ, especially by the time he is executed.

Not only that, but the way she is presented in the gospels seems to position her as an important figure. Every time a group of women is mentioned in the gospel of Mark, for example, it is Mary Magdalen who is mentioned first. In each of the four major gospels, her name is specifically mentioned in a way which — according to the historian Carla Ricci — "cannot be considered fortuitous." Her mention is deliberate and the importance which the writers place on her presence is clearly intentional. So how was she transformed from an important follower of Christ into a woman whose name became a byword for a prostitute?

We already know that the view of Mary Magdalen as a repentant prostitute is not supported by the gospels. She is not mentioned anywhere else in the canonical bible (though she does make an appearance in a number of the books which were supposedly cut from inclusion). Scholars have traced the sullying of the reputation of Mary Magdalen back to Pope Gregory I. In 591, he issued a claim which conflated both Mary Magdalen and an unnamed sinner in the bible. He formed what is known today as a "composite Mary." This meant that she now would carry a reputation for the sins of many other people who are not named in the text itself. Gradually, the seven demons that were said to be expunged from her body by Jesus came to represent the seven capital sins and, soon enough, Mary Magdalen was being condemned as a representation of lust and covetousness.

But there is a hidden history of Mary Magdalen. As well as her unfair corruption by the Catholic Church, there is said to have been a number of other sources from the time that the gospels were written that position her as being far more important to Christianity. Known as the Gnostic gospels, there are a number of books which were not included in the bible. While Matthew, Mark, Luke, and John are the accepted four gospels, there are also accounts from other apostles, such as Philip. For one reason or another, they were not chosen to be included in the 'official' biblical canon. They had been pieced together today as the Apocrypha and few traces of their messages can be read. Perhaps most importantly, we have discovered that there was — at one time or another — a Gospel of Mary.

The Gospel of Mary differs from the main texts in a number of ways. Firstly, it places a higher importance on the role of women in the early Christian Church. It is thought that the book was written at the same time as the Gospel of Philip (also in the Apocrypha) though the fragments we have of the Gospel of Mary date from around the third century. It is generally accepted that the Mary of the title is Mary Magdalen. Indeed, in the course of the gospel, there is the admission that Mary was preferred by Jesus compared to all of the other disciples. As well as Peter admitting that Jesus loved Mary "more than the rest of woman," Levi suggests that "the Saviour … loved [Mary Magdalen] more than us."

But there are other mentions of Mary in the Apocrypha. In the Gospel of Philip, she is described using the Greek word for partner, companion, or comrade. Variously, Philip describes how the affection shown to her by Jesus caused jealousy and annoyance among the other disciples, as well as mentioning that Christ used to "kiss her often." It is references such as these that form the basis for one of the key conceits of the Priory of Sion.

As we have seen earlier in this book, *The Holy Blood and the Holy Grail* works hard to establish the theory that Jesus bore children. According to their theory, it was Mary Magdalen who not only mothered the divine bloodline, but was actually Jesus's wife. Given as evidence are facts such as the preference the apostles seem to give her in the gospels, that Jesus would appear to her in private as the first person he visited when coming back to life, and mentions such as that in the Gospel of Philip which seem to describe a romantic relationship. They argue that it would have been perfectly natural for a Jewish man in the Near East at the time to have a wife and to have children, so much so that it was not worth mentioning in the text other than in passing. Mary Magdalen, they argue, was actually the wife of Jesus Christ.

And this is where one of the more conspiratorial aspects of the book comes to the forefront. It is argued in *The Holy Blood and the Holy Grail* (as well as *The Da Vinci Code*) that Mary Magdalen became an enemy of the Catholic Church. We have already noted the apparent jealousy that the other disciples were said to feel towards her, while her demonization by the church is said to be a part of a Catholic conspiracy to maintain power. Her reputation was sullied in order to discredit her and to discredit the potential bloodline of Jesus Christ. Whereas a descendant of Jesus might be a threat to the Pope as God's representation on Earth, the child of a prostitute merited little attention. The campaign against Mary Magdalen was not just an attempt to reassert patriarchal beliefs through the medium of a religious text, but it was an active attempt to discredit the one threat to the Catholic Church's position. In that respect, they certainly succeeded.

Or did they? If nothing else, books such as *The Holy Blood and the Holy Grail* and *The Da Vinci Code* have prompted a mainstream reappraisal of the identity of Mary Magdalen. As we have seen, it is now possible to go online and search for more information on subjects related to the Priory of Sion. If, when searching online, one discovers the tangents and the associated ideas, then they might come across the numerous sources which state the claim about the real nature of Mary Magdalen. While she might not have been the wife of Jesus Christ (and her being linked to the Priory of Sion is yet another aspect of that hoax), there are sources and academic works out there which discuss the reputation and the changing attitudes towards this figure over the years. In prompting people to learn more about Mary Magdalen, provably false works about the Priory of Sion can point readers and audiences towards a small kernel of the truth. In that respect, at least, it seems that the Priory of Sion is retroactively doing a great deal to promote Mary Magdalen.

While they might not be protecting a fictitious bloodline, they are in fact doing something in encouraging people to delve deeper into the actual truth behind one of the bible's most mysterious figures. In a manner nobody ever expected, books such as *The Holy Blood and the Holy Grail* have managed to alter public opinion on Mary Magdalen, or at least begin a gradual movement towards a reassessment of who she actually was. As such, it might even be possible to claim that the Priory of Sion have partly succeeded in their goal, even after having been proven as a complete hoax.

The Grand Masters

Another core part of the myth of the Priory of Sion is the exaltation of the supposed Grand Masters. In creating the backstory for the existence of the Priory, Plantard and his fellow hoaxers very carefully put together a list of people whom they considered to be potential leaders of a secret, anti-Catholic organization. They even gave the position a title, naming the Grand Masters as the Nautonnier, which is an Old French word that translates roughly as 'navigator.' In esoteric circles, the title of Nautonnier has variously be translated as Grand Master, hence the title that is given in both *The Da Vinci Code* and *The Holy Blood and the Holy Grail*.

The way in which the list of previous Grand Masters was put together was one of the more devious aspects of the Priory of Sion hoax and it is one which has often gotten the most attention from the public. Using the assumed name Philippe Toscan du Plantier, Pierre Plantard painstakingly assembled his list which spans from 1188 right up to the 1960s. The list was included in the *Dossiers Secrets* d'Henri Lobineau, which was the document he and his team hid inside the National Library of France and waited for people to discover.

The list was complex in its creation. It should seem an obvious point that each person included and mentioned by name was dead by the time Plantard put pen to paper. This meant that there was no one living who could deny their involvement. If any family member or biographer spoke up and questioned the inclusion of any one particular person, Plantard and his co-conspirators could quite easily fall back on the reasoning that the Priory of Sion was a secret society and that there was little chance of the Grand Master himself telling people of its existence.

The list includes some of the most famous artists and thinkers in European history, though it is not entirely without a basis. In fact, all but two of the names that are on the list can actually be found on the list of members of the Ancient Mystical Order Rosae Crucis, another fabricated secret religious society which was becoming increasingly famous in France at the time of Plantard's writing. In addition, many of the people on the list have been noted for possessing a vague interest in the existence of the occult, so their inclusion plays on the expectations and notions many members of the public already possess.

As a point of interest, it should be noted that Plantard created an interesting piece of lore in writing the *Dossiers Secrets*. According to him, the Priory of Sion and the Knights Templar shared a common Grand Master for a long time. That was up until 1188, when a schism occurred. Following this, each society had a different leader. Plantard even tied this into a real historical event, known as the Cutting of the Elm. This referred to a diplomatic incident between the English and the French monarchies, known to commemorate the negotiations between the Franks and the Normans. While the English had stood in the shade of the tree, the French had been made to suffer under the light of the sun. Following the close of the talks, the French king demanded that the tree be cut down. This was a sign that the English would be shown no quarter should they continue to disagree. Through reasons not made explicitly clear, this historical event had an impact on the Grand Masters of the Priory of Sion. Little touches such as this are just one way in which Plantard sought to lend his creation a sense of historical legitimacy, offering readers just enough fact to allow them to form their own conclusions.

In all, the list is comprised of 26 men. In chronological order, they are:

- Jean de Gisors
- Marie de Saint-Clair
- Guillaume de Gisors
- Edouard de Bar
- Jeanne de Bar
- Jean de Saint-Clair
- Blanche d'Évreux
- Nicolas Flamel
- René d'Anjou
- Iolande de Bar
- Sandro Filipepi
- Léonard da Vinci
- Connétable de Bourbon
- Ferdinand de Gonzague
- Louis de Nevers
- Robert Fludd
- J. Valentin Andrea
- Robert Boyle
- Isaac Newton
- Charles Radclyffe
- Charles de Lorraine
- Maximilian de Lorraine
- Charles Nodier
- Victor Hugo
- Claude Debussy
- And Jean Cocteau

A quick look through the list reveals a number of famous and less famous figures. Leonardo da Vinci and Isaac Newton are two which immediately catch the eye — surely the reason why Dan Brown titled his book *The Da Vinci Code* — while members such as Robert Fludd and Edouard de Bar are certainly much less famous. It's a clever tactic, one used by the person who created the lists on which Plantard based his own. By masking attention grabbing names amid other less dramatic (though credible in their own right) names, it brings a great sense of legitimacy to the list. It's a sleight of hand trick, applied to a religious hoax.

But that is not the end of the matter. There are further documents created by Plantard that expand on his list of Grand Masters. One of these is named Le Cercle d'Ulysse and it was also a falsified and planted piece of so-called evidence. It mentions that Francois Ducaud-Bourget is the latest in the long name of Grand Masters. But Francois Ducaud-Bourget was not just another name. In fact, it was the name of a man whom Plantard knew personally. He had been a Catholic priest and was known as having been something of a traditionalist. Plantard had worked for the man as a sexton during the Second World War. Plantard named him as the Grand Master following the death of Jean Cocteau. It's an example of the hoaxer drawing the circle in tightly around himself. Alongside claims Plantard made of having Merovingian heritage, he was using events from his own life as a means of providing foundations for an elaborate hoax.

But it did not take long for the *Dossiers Secrets* to be exposed as fraudulent. While many tests are available that can ascertain the age of a particular document or piece of paper (useful when assessing purportedly ancient sources), this was not relevant to the *Dossiers Secrets*. With it running all the way up to the modern day, there was little need for Plantard to claim it was anything other than an updated list belonging to an ancient order. But that did not mean that it was not easily proven wrong. It was traced back to Plantard's hand and, after other members of the group confessed to the hoax, it was not long before the lie was exposed (at least in France.) But during the early stages of the exposed hoax, Plantard kept decidedly quiet. He was very much involved in every aspect of the conspiracy and it should have been no surprise to anyone to see that Plantard was able to produce a second, revised list of Grand Masters. During one 1989 revival of the story of the Priory of Sion, Plantard presented his new list to the public. The first list, he knew, was discredited, so the second was a slightly more reserved affair. Gone are names such as Leonardo da Vinci and Isaac Newton, while the new list seems to have a decidedly more French orientation. What's more, it only traces the Grand Masters back to the 1600s, making less grand claims than the first *Dossiers Secrets*. By 1993, however, this list was also confirmed as a hoax.

The fame of the Grand Masters is one of the most memorable aspects of the Priory of Sion. When people are investigating the mystery for themselves, one of the major points of focus is the celebrity of those involved. If it was enough to welcome in some of the greatest thinkers, the hoax suggests, then surely there must be some credibility to the matter. In doing so, the hoax plays on the famous intellect of the purported members and borrows legitimacy from their actual accomplishments to make the Priory of Sion seem more real.

While this is perhaps the headline-grabbing feature of the Priory of Sion (thanks to *The Da Vinci Code*, it is at least as famous as the idea of a divine bloodline), it is likely that the list of the Grand Masters attracted far too much attention. When the organization was nothing more than the clandestine protectors of a conspiratorial idea, then it was almost impossible to disprove in any complete capacity. But the involvement of such famous names adds yet another way of disproving Plantard's elaborate hoax. Various scholars, researchers, and academics have demonstrated with consummate ease why various members of the list could not be involved for reasons such as geographic location, ideological inclination, or simply that they were dead at the time they were meant to be heading up a secret society. In that respect, Plantard seems to have overreached in this ambition. The people he hoped to involve in the Priory of Sion were almost too famous for his own good.

The Da Vinci Code

Along with the fairly easy dismissal of the celebrity Grand Masters, it becomes easy to question yet another appealing aspect of the Priory of Sion: the idea that they hid clues in the medieval, Renaissance, and Enlightenment art in order to hint at the secret they kept hidden. If we know that Leonardo da Vinci was in no way involved with the Priory of Sion, it becomes relatively straightforward to dismiss the idea that he hid clues to the organization's existence within his artwork.

The idea already fails to hold up under close examination. The concept of hiding clues inside some of the world's most popular pieces of art seems reasonable enough, until it becomes clear that these clues are said to point towards the existence of a secret society. Any organization that truly wanted to remain in the dark and away from the mainstream would be better served by hiding false clues or even no clues at all in the various works. However, thanks to the fact that the list was proven to be false, it can easily be dismissed.

The notion does point towards why the Priory of Sion has become an enduring myth, however. One need only look at *The Da Vinci Code* for confirmation. *The Da Vinci Code* was released in 2003. By this point in time, the Priory of Sion and everything written in *The Holy Blood and the Holy Grail* had already been proven false. It was a known hoax, though perhaps not a famous one. The way in which the book presented the existence of the Priory managed to convince a certain section of its readership that there might be some truth behind the conspiracy. In fact, it followed many of the same steps we have already covered in this book and attributed to Baigent, Leigh, and Lincoln.

But what *The Da Vinci Code* did do was introduce the idea of the Priory of Sion to a new generation. More than a decade had passed between the release of Dan Brown's book and *The Holy Blood and the Holy Grail*. This meant that there was a huge number of people to whom the Priory of Sion was not a known quantity. There were also those who had heard of many of the theories, but had perhaps not heard of the proven falsities that had come out in the wake of the hoax's reveal. That meant that Dan Brown was able to recapture some of the intrigue and fascination that so managed to catch people the first time around. In doing so, he was even able to make a great deal of money.

And, typically, that is where the myth of the Priory of Sion returns. Even though it has already been proven to be false, at least three distinct groups of people have managed to make money using the idea. There is the original band of French hoaxers, there are the authors of *The Holy Blood and the Holy Grail*, and there is Dan Brown and his publishers. Either knowingly (in the case of the original hoaxers) or unknowingly (supposedly in the remaining cases) the conspiracy has been sold to the public on a number of occasions. It has been used to revive the flagging interests of a hotel, to sell a non-fiction book, and to popularise a book and film tie-in of the story of an art professor who solves crimes.

That is without mentioning the scores of people who have written companion books, filmed exploratory documentaries, or even those who offer tours around religious sites in the south of France. On many levels, the Priory of Sion has proved to be a profitable venture. And for such a supposedly elaborate conspiracy, perhaps that is the real truth. Rather than the Catholic Church waging a war against the descendants of Jesus Christ, the real conspiracy is those who hope to make money from the idea of the Priory of Sion. From websites to jewelery, non-fiction to fiction, people have learned about the story and then hoped to pass it along to others. The real clue hidden in the art work does not point towards the existence of the Priory of Sion, but rather towards its profitability.

Conclusion

Typically, this would be the place to end this book. The hoax has been revealed, the truth outed. The nature of the Priory of Sion has been discussed and its reasoning detailed. But that is not the final chapter of the story. Despite the huge amount of evidence to the contrary, there are still those who are convinced that the Priory of Sion is a legitimate organization and one which still guards a secret to this day. But after everything we have seen and all of the confessions that have been made, how can we possibly believe that someone could seriously invest in this idea?

Some people have pointed to *The Da Vinci Code* as being a source of these problems. However, unlike the original *The Holy Blood and the Holy Grail*, Dan Brown's book did not sit in the history section of the book store. Even though the author opened his book with a claim that everything contained within was true, it was still nestled neatly in the fiction section. There was a reasonable amount of doubt that could be attributed to the information inside, even if the book did perhaps believe in its own mythology. Indeed, Brown's choice of antagonist is telling. While people such as Baigent, Leigh, and Lincoln have previously suggested the existence of natural enemies for the Priory of Sion, Brown decided to go a different way entirely. In the Messianic Legacy, Baigent et al suggested that the enemy of the Priory might actually be the Sovereign Order of Malta, tracing potential disagreements back to the Crusades. While it was built on as rocky a foundation as the rest of their work, it did at least feature a reasonable (if poorly researched) suggestion. But Brown ignored that. Instead, he selected as his antagonist the Catholic sect Opus Dei. Though controversial in their own right, Opus Dei had never once been linked with the Priory of Sion in any capacity. It was entirely conjecture, put down to poetic license. In ways such as these, it's easy to see that *The Da Vinci Code* is discredited without too much trouble.

The serious allegations that the Priory of Sion still exists are found firmly out of the non-fiction section. Much like *The Holy Blood and the Holy Grail*, these books often purport to be serious historical investigations but fail to measure up to the required research standards. One such example *is The Sion Revelation*, written by Lynn Picknett and Clive Prince. The subtitle of the book suggests that readers will learn "the truth about the guardians of Christ's sacred bloodline." The two authors are not without previous work on this kind of topic. Indeed, their 1997 book *The Templar Revelation* is said to have been the chief source used by Dan Brown for ideas about the interplay between the Knights Templar and Leonardo da Vinci. However, *The Sion Revelation* goes much further.

In the book, the authors accept that Pierre Plantard forged much of the evidence for the existence of the Priory of Sion before 1956. This, they say, was deliberate. It was intended to muddy the waters, to blur the lines between reality and fiction. It created a red herring in the minds of the public, who would now know that the Priory of Sion was a hoax. It was a distraction, and a successful one, orchestrated by both Plantard and the people who oversaw his actions.

Instead, they believe that the Priory of Sion was nothing more than a cover organization for a modern political movement. The group hopes to unite the nations of Europe into a new world power, much like the Priory was said to have been doing for years. But their activities are secret. In setting up such a complex hoax, Plantard and the rest of the real Priory were able to distract the public from their efforts. It is a real conspiracy, hidden behind a forged conspiracy that was supposed to be real. But like many examples of Priory of Sion-orientated literature found in both book stores and on the internet, there is little to no evidence. Nothing compelling is put forward other than run-of-the-mill conspiratorial ideas. Movements such as these rob the Priory of Sion of its original distinguishing characteristic (the religious concepts) and turn it into another shadowy organization bent on taking over the world. The legacy of the Priory of Sion might be many things, but one of the worst is the latest wave of poorly informed, poorly researched books which claim to know the real truth. While Plantard and his team were cunning in their hoax, the only remaining adherents to theory of the Priory's existence have robbed it of all cleverness. By now, the Priory of Sion is just another entry in the list of standard conspiracy theories. Easily disproven and easily forgotten, the modern mentions of the Priory pale in comparison to previous efforts.

And that is the state of the Priory of Sion today. In this current climate, they occupy the same mental space as the Illuminati or the Assassins. They are blamed for global (or more specifically, European) conspiracies despite the lack of attention paid to their past. Now functioning in the same way as the Illuminati or the New World Order, any legitimate dismissal of their activities is attributed to false agents and even more levels of conspiracy. But as much as we might have wanted the story of the Priory of Sion to be true, these days we know it was nothing more than an elaborate lie. For now, the various ideas put forward by Plantard, Baigent, Lincoln, and Leigh will be consigned to the forgotten histories. For such a contrived construction, this might be more than anyone ever expected.

Further Reading

Baigent, M., Leigh, R. and Lincoln, H. (1982). *Holy Blood, Holy Grail*. New York: Delacorte Press.
Baigent, M., Leigh, R. and Lincoln, H. (1987). *The Messianic Legacy*. New York: Holt.
Brown, D. (2003). *The Da Vinci Code*. New York: Doubleday.
Chaumeil, J. (2010). *The Priory of Sion*. London: Avalonia.
Howells, R. (2011). *Inside the Priory of Sion*. London: Watkins Pub.
King James Version popular award Bible. (2001). London: HarperCollins.
Picknett, L. and Prince, C. (2006). *The Sion Revelation*. New York: Simon & Schuster.

About the Author

Conrad Bauer is passionate about everything paranormal, unexplained, mysterious, and terrifying. It comes from his childhood and the famous stories his grandfather used to tell the family during summer vacation camping trips. He vividly remembers his grandfather sitting around the fire with new stories to tell everyone who would gather around and listen. His favorites were about the paranormal, including ghost stories, haunted houses, strange places, and paranormal occurrences.

Bauer is an adventurous traveler who has gone to many places in search of the unexplained and paranormal. He has been researching the paranormal and what scares people for more than four decades. He also loves to dig into period of history that are still full of mysteries, being an avid reader of the mystic secret societies that have mark history and remain fascinating and legendary throughout the times. He has accumulated a solid expertise and knowledge that he now shares through his books with his readers and followers.

Conrad, now retired, lives in the countryside in Ireland with his wife and two dogs.

More Books from Conrad Bauer

Y

Printed in Great Britain
by Amazon